Kansas To Can-Can

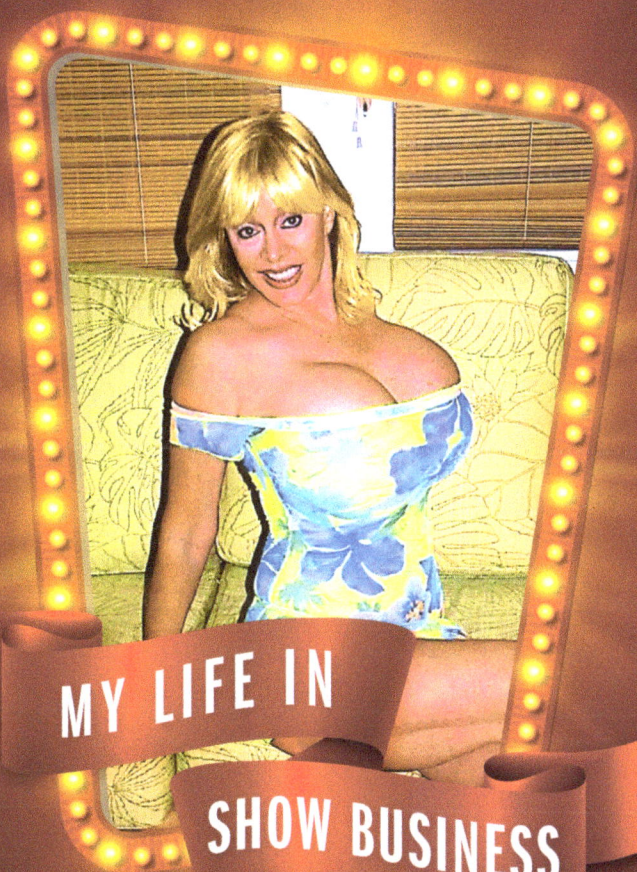

MY LIFE IN SHOW BUSINESS

STAR OF STAGE, SCREEN, AND MAGAZINE

PATTY PLENTY

Contents

My upbringing in conservative Wichita and my early dancing and acting career

My Childhood and Family Background
- father served in WWII on a submarine
- father as top executive
- mother performed with June Taylor dancers
- interesting stories of family life
- dance training starting at the age of 4
- difficulty adjusting to wealthy suburban Wichita school

Early Dance Experience in Wichita

- talented dancer at an early age
- competed in regional contests

Early Professional Experience Outside of Wichita

- lead Cancan dancer at Moulin Rouge in Vienna
- popular exotic dancer at clubs around the country
- created my own road show
- traveled with my beloved cat Susan B Anthony
- youngest dancer ever with Folies Bergere at Ttopicana

First Movie - The Gypsy Moths

- contract with Metro Goldwyn Mayer
- affair with Burt Lancaster
- affair with director John Frankenheimer
- impressions of Gene Hackman and Deborrah Kerr

Second Movie - *Going In Style*

- cameo role in original 1979 film
- re-make in 2017 with new cast

Miss Nude Ohio

- why I decided to compete
- difficult dance routine
- strange interview on local TV

Working in Cleveland

- Stage Door Johnnies and the Theatrical
- affairs with Bob Crane and David Miller

An insider's view of the Las Vegas entertainment business

My Relationship with Singer and Comedian Steve Rossi
- famous comedy partnership with Marty Allen
- we performed in several shows together including Burlesque '79
- lived at my home with me and husband Jack Hunt
- his early career and sponsorship by Mae West
- how he got his stage name

Relationships with a Multitude of Stars
- long term friendship with Phyllis McGuire
- impressions of Neil Sedaka, Georgie Jessel, Tom Jones, and Liberace
- history of the Rat Pack and my dealings with them

Casino Mogul Bob Stupak
- my turbulent relationship with him
- performed as star attraction at Vegas World and the Stratosphere
- my bad relationship with the other dancers
- publicity stunts
- his tragic end

Steve Rossi Funeral
- opportunity to meet old acquantances
- reunion with producer Jay Harvey

Frequent Visits to Vegas
- Pamplemousse French restaurant
- Piero's Itaian restaurant

A hilarious account of how I met and married seven wealthy eccentric men

Introduction
- how I compare to Elizabeth Taylor and Zsa Zsa Gabor
- how the movie *Magnificent Seven* relates to this chapter

First Husband – Tom Wright
- drummer in local Wichita band
- breakup over his lack of ambition

Second Husband – John Henry
- successful stock broker
- conflict over his handling of money
- my strange relationship with his former wife

Third Husband – George Etherington
- actual nephew of President Dwight D Eisenhower
- his extreme generosity and his efforts to win my affection
- surprising ending of our marriage

Fourth Husband – Jack Hunt

- how he acquired his name as an orphan
- our first encounter
- our travels to exotic locales
- his expensive gifts
- his successful career in real estate
- why my career ended marriage

Fifth Husband – Michael Flores

- engaged to daughter of Rita Hayworth and Orson Welles
- how we met
- how I tricked him on a flight to the Bahamas to see Foreman-Ali fight
- our stormy relationship that went to extremes
- his conflict with Steve Wynn over the property behind Mirage
- his financial and personal relationship with Bob Stupak

Sixth Husband – Lynn Thomas

- successful business owner despite serious handicaps
- intolerable jealous nature
- his strange behavior in divorce court

Seventh Husband - Lew Warren

- talented ventriloquist and work-a-holic
- how he influenced my career
- his high risk lifestyle and eccentric behavior

- his financial irresponsibiity
- his strange relationship with our daughter Glennel

The lurid details of my escapades on and off the screen as a porn star.

Introduction to the Business
- how my chance encounter with Veronica Hart changed history
- how I got a lucrative contract with Caballero
- difficulty in adapting to my first porn movie *Bodaciou TaTas*

Getting on Top
- life and career of iconic porn star Ron Jeremy
- my wild adventures with porn star Kitten Natividad
- the pros and cons of an adult film career
- engaging in a swinger lifestyle
- my starring role in my second film *Stiff Competition*

Success as a Mature Star
- setting trends as a mature star
- humorous account of my botched induction into *Legends of Erotica*
- my current involvement in the business

My exciting life among the rich and famous in Malibu

Living with the Stars
- friend of Hugh Hefner and frequent guest at the Playboy Mansion
- long friendship with Olivia Newton-John
- daughter going to school with children of the stars
- friend of Clippers owner Donald Sterling
- outdoor activities with versatile actor John Philip Law
- working out at the gym with Matthew McConaughey
- wild antics of Gerry Wersh who worked for Herb Alpert

My Homes in Malibu
- romantic relationship with wealthy developer Rob McCloud
- living downstairs in same condo with Sam Walton's daughter
- living next to Shirley MacLaine
- my Asian leopard cats, Henry and Isaac

Trouble with the Law
- beating speeding tickets
- attending traffic school for DUI in Beverly Hills with Robert Downey Jr.

Personal Product Promotions

- how I was able to successfully market breast enlargement cream
- why the FDA banned the sale of this product
- marketing Patty Plenty wine
- marketing Patty Plenty watches

Fanfare Studios

- starting my own digital production company in Malibu
- producing and selling adult videos
- ten year long battle with the IRS and how I managed to remove lien

My active life in Hawaii and my overseas adventures

Move to Hawaii

- setting up my daughter on Maui
- my beach house on North Shore of Oahu
- relationship with Buzzy Hong
- political activity
- house on South Shore
- group tap dancing, trips to the gym, hiking and swimming

Taking Care of Business

- running my popular website

- active on Social Media
- prior performances in Guyana and Surinam

Latin American Cruises

- solo flight to Rio and stay at the Sheraton overlooking the beach
- learning to tight rope
- Argentine food, music, and art
- return luxury flight on Emirates Airlines
- cruise to Cuba with mother
- meeting the people of Cuba
- cruise to Pacific Coast of South America
- passing through the Panama Canal
- seventy thousand dollar "engagement" watch
- lost in Lima

Conclusion

- transatlantic cruise to Europe
- plan to appear in one woman show, *Patty Plenty Live*

Illustrations

Chapter Two: What Happens in Vegas

Chapter Three: The Seven Dwarfs Or The Magnificent Seven?

Chapter Four: The Nifty Fifties

Chapter Five: A Place in the Sun

Chapter Six: A Stranger in Paradise

—⊶⊷—

I dedicate my book in loving memory to my father Glenn, to my mother Connie who is still active at the age of 93, and to my beloved daughter Glennel who has recently married.

—⊶⊷—

Introduction

I AM BUSTY blond legendary film star Patty Plenty. I have appeared in both mainstream films including *The Gypsy Moths* with Burt Lancaster and Gene Hackman, and adult films including *Bodacious Tatas* with Ron Jeremy and Kitten Natividad.

In addition, I enjoyed a long and successful career as a headline singer and dancer on the Las Vegas Strip. Many of my routines were a reenactment of old burlesque. Not only did my success bring financial rewards and plenty of publicity in the society columns, but I had the opportunity to live and work with some of the biggest stars and high rollers in Las Vegas.

My book *Kansas to Cancan* presents a provocative portrait of my life in show business from an insider's point of view. I reveal my steamy affairs with director John Frankenheimer, producer

Jay Harvey, singer and comedian Steve Rossi, and casino mogul Bob Stupak, to name a few.

One of the chapters "The Seven Dwarfs or the Magnificent Seven?" recounts my tumultuous seven marriages to some very rich and eccentric men. I tell some incredible and amusing stories such as the time I boarded a plane bound for the Bahamas in disguise to fool my future husband. Another chapter, "The Nifty Fifties" is the story of my long porn star career in which I give lurid details of my exploits on and off the screen.

Other chapters relate my childhood in Wichita, my early dance career with the Folies Bergere and the Moulin Rouge, my life in Malibu beside a host of celebrities including Olivia Newton-John and Shirley MacLaine, and my efforts to market such diverse products as my own brand of wine, and a breast enlargement cream that was later banned by the FDA. Embedded throughout this book are dozens of photos and promotions from by extensive personal collection that will greatly enhance the reading experience.

I have also provided some little-known facts in the history of Las Vegas such as the real story behind the feud between casino magnate Steve Wynn, and my former husband, Michael Flores over the property behind the Mirage casino, as well as the origin of the Rat Pack.

For several years, I wrote a column for Cheri Magazine out of New York as well as other adult magazines. Therefore, I gained an enormous amount of publicity which greatly enhanced my career as well as my mail order business. I appeared on the cover of so many of the top men's magazines that I dominated the newsstands from coast to coast and around the world.

I would like to thank my assistant writer, Norman Belli, for his invaluable service. In addition to creating the titles and preparing an outline, he was heavily involved in the writing and editing. He also conducted interviews with my only living former husband, Michael Flores, my friend and co-star, Kitten Natividad, my mother Connie, and my daughter Glennel.

I currently live in Hawaii where I maintain a home on the south shore just east of Waikiki and Diamond Head, and I continue to lead a very active social and business life. For many years, I have operated my website, https://www.pplease.com, to cater to my far flung fan base acquired over five decades.

Maid in Kansas

GIVEN MY UPBRINGING in conservative middle America in the 50's and 60's, it would have been hard to predict that I would someday become a world-famous porn star.

My father, Glenn, served on a submarine, the Barb, during World War II. He was only 17 when he joined the service so his mother had to sign a waiver. Ironically, he had to promise her that he would never serve on a submarine. His best friend on the submarine was an eighteen-year-old baker named Russ Elliman. By some act of fate, their grandchildren, Russ Elliman's grandson, and my daughter Glennel, would meet by chance, become friends, and surf together in Malibu some sixty years later.

A movie, *Thunder Below* was later made based on the exploits of Admiral Fluckey, who commanded the sub. Both my mother and father were interviewed before the movie was produced to learn about their experiences during the war.

My father started out after the war as an assistant repairman working on toasters. However, my mother insisted that he attend college and get a degree, so he would no longer have to carry a lunch bucket. After receiving a degree in Nuclear Physics from Wichita State University, he became a Vice President at Kansas Gas and Electric and helped build the first nuclear power plant in all of Kansas. It took him thirteen years to complete two degrees because he worked during the day and attended school at night.

My mother, Connie, performed with the June Taylor dancers and appeared on the Jackie Gleason show. My father was very traditional, and was displeased that she was working outside the home, which ended her brief career.

Young Mother and Daddy

Walking in Wichita

When I was only two, our family moved to Hawaii where we lived for about eighteen months. I have always loved the ocean, having lived in land-locked Kansas for so many years.

I felt fortunate that I was an only child. My parents used to say that I was lucky that I didn't have any sisters or brothers because I didn't have to share my toys. Since I always had plenty of toys, that argument just didn't register with me.

We were a typical middle class family, living on $200 a week, which was good money in those days. We were probably better off than most of our neighbors where both parents had to work. Unlike our neighbors, we were able to go on vacation every year, although we always had to borrow money to do it. We did a lot of mountain climbing at Longs Peak in Rocky Mountain National Park in Colorado. We would start up the mountain before sunrise and didn't come down off the mountain until almost sunset. We became quite experienced climbers and had all of the right equipment to avoid injury, and many climbers were actually killed. On one occasion, I slipped but was rescued by my father who caught me by one leg, while hanging in the air upside down.

Childhood Photos

Halloween in Hawaii

Most of my classmates in Wichita were Arab or Jewish, so that I was required to attend school with some very rich and snobby kids. To make matters worse, I was not a good student. The only subject that I did well in was typing.

I went to school with a girl whose parents bred Arabian horses for Hollywood, as well as other kids from families in the oil business. On one occasion, a science teacher went around the room and asked an unusual question, "What do your parents own?" One girl said that her mom and dad owned Macys. Another kid replied that his mom and dad owned Henry's, an upscale retail store similar to Nieman Marcus. When it was my turn, I said that my father worked at Kansas Gas and Electric.

When I was asked if he owned it, I told them that I didn't think so, trying to fit into this snobby environment. After I stayed with one wealthy family for dinner, I came running home full of excitement to tell my mother, "They are so rich that they eat bacon with a knife and fork!"

I became a Bluebird and a Campfire Girl which I considered better than the Brownies and the Girl Scouts. I still have my uniform decorated with beads which I earned by selling candy door to door. The boys would join the Indian Guides considered superior to the Boy Scouts. My very first boyfriend, Mike Kaufman, made money by selling golf balls that he either collected from the nearly golf course - or stole outright. My first serious date was a boy who showed up barefoot and no shirt to take me to the movies, which really upset my mother. However, he was the same boy who later took me to the prom in fancy attire. Maybe his parents had straightened him out.

I began taking dancing lessons at the age of four and continued up to age eighteen. I spent nine months a year in intensive training with three months off for the summer. I really enjoyed tap dancing but also worked hard on ballet, jazz and acrobatics. All of my relatives would come to see my recitals. In addition, I would practice tap dancing for hours and hours on the porch in front of the neighbors, who would laugh considering me to be

a big showoff. I had quite an audience since there were twelve
small World War II style houses on both sides of the road.

Early Dance Performance

Dawn of a Dance Duo

When I was about thirteen, my parents told me that they could not really afford paying for my lessons, and that I should probably quit. I told them that I had no intention of quitting, and that they had no right to even suggest it.

I had become a very talented dancer in Wichita at an early age. I was in constant demand and appeared all over the city for the VFW, the American Legion, nursing homes - you name it. I even produced and directed *West Side Story* at one of the local high schools. I was now ready to venture out on the road to perform in various routines all over the country.

I entered a regional tap dancing contest in Terre Haute, Indiana and won second place. I don't know why I didn't finish first – it could have been the routine or maybe just politics.

As soon as I finished high school in Wichita, I contracted a job through the Wichita School of Fine Arts, and went out to Vegas to work as an acrobat with the Folies Bergere at the Tropicana. No one had ever asked for my age, so at 17, I became the youngest dancer ever to be accepted, but they still allowed me to sit at the bar. In those days in Vegas, you could get way with almost anything. The Vegas show had its roots in the original Folies Bergere theater, which opened in Paris in 1869 and first featured a nude showgirl in 1918. The Vegas show offered dazzling productions for almost fifty years, but recently closed in 2009.

Vintage French Poster

Poor Butterfly Routine

I even entered the Miss Nude Ohio contest in order to gain additional publicity. I won by performing a difficult dance routine with a patriotic theme that required a lot of high kicks and intricate foot work. I wore a costume emblazoned with stars and stripes, along with a top hat reminiscent of Uncle Sam. My task was made easier when my main competitor, who was a very talented Country and Western singer, was forced by circumstance to perform without her band. Therefore, I was able to win the first prize of $10,000, but it only covered a fraction of my expenses. Just a single costume could cost as much, and I had at least a dozen outfits. I also spent about $20,000 on lights and a light man pulling a trailer. Afterwards, I did a somewhat strange interview on a local network in which I was asked by a woman reporter, "Isn't it difficult to hide a few extra pounds when you are completely nude?"

I worked the Vaudeville and Burlesque circuits all over the country – North, South, East, and West. I even worked in small remote clubs like Grumpy's in Amarillo, Texas.

When I drove with my mother all the way to Florida to appear in a night club there, local thugs had broken in and shot up the place just before my matinee performance was to begin, and I was warned to lock myself inside of my dressing room. However, I could not be deterred, and my mother was shocked to see me perform among broken glass and shattered debris.

I then entered the next stage of my career when I first met famed Hollywood director, John Frankenheimer, at the 49 a Go Go in Wichita, where I was working for a short time. His numerous and highly popular feature films and plays for television were notable for creating psychological dilemmas for his characters, and a strong sense of place. He was very handsome and from a very rich family. He directed one of his movies, *Grand Prix*, based on his own experience since he had grown up in Europe, and had driven a Ferrari as a teenager, becoming familiar with the auto racing circuit.

Frankenheimer On Set

He was planning on using the exact replica of the club in a new movie, *The Gypsy Moths*, even to the point of duplicating a tear in the ceiling. It is the story of three barn storming skydivers and their effect on a small Midwestern town, with the main characters played by Burt Lancaster, Gene Hackman, Deborah Kerr, and Sheree North. The movie focuses on the differences in values between the town folk and the hard-living skydivers.

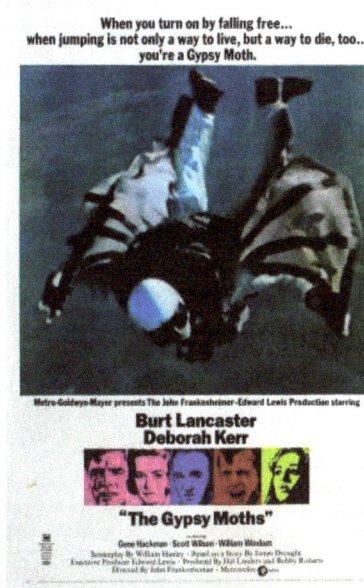

When you turn on by falling free...
when jumping is not only a way to live, but a way to die, too...
you're a Gypsy Moth.

Metro-Goldwyn-Mayer presents The John Frankenheimer-Edward Lewis Production starring

Burt Lancaster
Deborah Kerr

"The Gypsy Moths"

Gene Hackman · Scott Wilson · William Windom

Promotion for *The Gypsy Moths*

John considered using me as a body double for Deborah Kerr in a nude love scene with Burt Lancaster, but thought that I might upstage siren Sheree North. However, after some initial testing, he offered me the part of a topless dancer instead, but planned to film me mostly from the neck down. He then told me, "Patty, I want you to come to Hollywood to sign a two year contract with Metro-Goldwyn-Mayer, and I want you to attend the Jeff Starkey Acting School." I was very excited since MGM was a huge enterprise at that time in the

60's and 70's. He also helped me get my Screen Actors Guild membership.

During the next six months, I did a number of bit parts for the studio, and also developed a romantic relationship with John. He was very charming, quite a gentleman – and a very good lover! My affair with him was one of the highlights of my entire life. One day, he pulled me into his magnificent office, put me on his lap behind his beautiful expensive desk, and told me that he loved me so very much and wanted to do the very best for me. However, he would be honest with me, and confessed that he could never marry me because he was still in love with his wife, who had the unusual name of Evans Evans, and he would never get a divorce.

I was quite surprised by his advances, and at age 19, not looking for a permanent commitment. At that time in Hollywood, the casting couch was the established path to an acting career, and I was merely adapting to the decadent ways of Tinsel Town. He bought me a number of expensive gifts including my first mink coat. When I was asked how I got the coat, I replied, "I got the coat the same way the minks did – by screwing."

When we began shooting the film, I naturally became familiar with the cast. Deborah Kerr was a kind and respectable British lady who would invite me into her elaborately furnished dressing room to enjoy tea and crumpets. Every time Gene Hackman saw me, he would hug and kiss me. When I first flew first class out to California, and stopped to get my luggage, he was there to pick me up. I heard him yell out, "Patty, Patty Wright, come over here." Since Gene Hackman knew me, I was now an immediate star – and I looked the part. I was dressed to kill. Back then, you didn't travel without the hat and handbag, lizard shoes, Louis Vuitton hat box, and a suit to go with it.

One day, I got a mysterious call from someone who asked me to go out with Burt Lancaster. I told the caller that I was not the right girl because I was already in tight with Frankenheimer. I was told not to worry about it, so I seized the opportunity, and met Burt at the Park Lane Towers, a luxurious high rise in Wichita for an erotic encounter. He was very intelligent, sophisticated, and cordial, and I was well rewarded for my efforts by the studio.

After the film was released, I became a local celebrity in my hometown of Wichita. I was invited to the prestigious Petroleum Club, a private hangout for Kansas oil executives. Being the prettiest girl in the room, I caught the attention of TV star, Monte Hall, host of *Let's Make a Deal*. Although he was considerably older than me, we partied and drank together all night long, and ended with a lot of monkey business.

Enjoying My New Celebrity with Monte Hall

I also worked in a full blown variety show called *Old Time Burlesque* with Charlie Vespia, Bob Mitchell, and Dusty Summers at the Joker Club in North Las Vegas. We did several burlesque routines including "The Crazy House." The club was located just across the street from the world famous strip club, the Palomino, which opened in 1969 and is still going strong. It is the only nude club in Vegas that offers alcohol, and it charges a premium for that privilege.

In 1979, I did a cameo role in *Going in Style,* a film written and directed by Martin Brest starring Art Carney, George Burns, and acting instructor Lee Strasberg. They played three senior citizens, living a boring life in Brooklyn, who decide to rob a bank. Not only do they manage to pull it off, but they used the stolen cash to win a fortune in Las Vegas. I played the part of an attractive girl at the Aladdin casino.

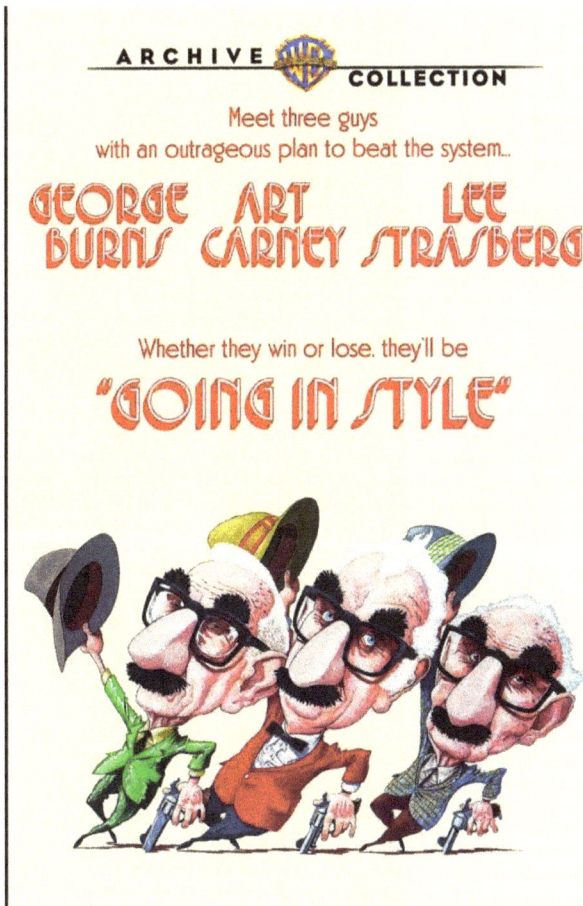

1979 Promotion for *Going In Style*

In April 2017, almost forty years later, a re-make of the movie opened in theaters around the country, with Alan Arkin, Morgan Freeman, and Michael Caine as the mischievous old men.

2017 Promotion for *Going in Style*

In the following years, I worked in major cities like New York and Chicago, being booked as a singer and dancer for one or two weeks at a time, four times a year. I quickly became popular with the rich and famous in all of these cities. I would stroll through the cosmetic department in Macy's in New York, and be greeted by the employees who would shout out. "Patty, how are you, we miss you! We miss you!" They would love me because I would spend $3000 to $4000 just in makeup in Macy's.

In Cleveland, I worked at an iconic strip club called Stage Door Johnnies. It was located in a seedy area on Prospect Street before the neighborhood was renovated. It was alongside an adult theater, and after the girls did the show, they went next door to solicit guys to enter private booths. There was still another theater nearby where the girls did a burlesque show, and then solicited the audience for bj's inside the men's room.

At Stage Door Johnnies, I met several big spenders including actor Bob Crane, the star of *Hogan's Heroes*, the long running TV series that spoofed a German POW camp that was loosely based on the movie, *Stalag 13*. He later earned notoriety for his wild affairs with scores of women, and these exploits were chronicled by his son Scotty in "The Faces of Bob Crane." I wasn't mentioned in the book, but I could have been since I was added to his tally after finding him to be very attractive.

In addition, there was the Theatrical, a huge bar in a beautiful expansive circular room, where all of the movie stars would gather.

Still another hot spot in downtown Cleveland near the Holiday Inn where I liked to hang out was Swingos, a rich upscale bar that attracted a wealthy clientele. It was named after a Greek immigrant who recognized that Cleveland was a major player in the national rock and roll industry, and that he could make a lot of money tapping into that market.

At Swingos, I met this wonderful slightly older good-looking man, David Miller, a multi-millionaire who owned Cleveland Iron and Steel, which he inherited from his father. I was having so much fun working in Cleveland and meeting rich and fabulous men, that I told David that I wanted to move there. He was astonished and told me, "Patty, are you crazy! Do you really want to leave your beautiful home in Las Vegas and move to friggin Cleveland, Ohio. It is cold here!" I replied, "Yes, I know, but you will buy me a lot of furs and jewelry." And he did, probably spending over $100,000 over the next two weeks. He bought me everything that you could imagine, except for the car that my husband had bought me. I drove into town in a

500SL, and drove out of town back to Vegas in a 500SL. Several years later he came to visit, and asked me to fix him up. I sent over a couple of thirty-year-old hookers who looked more like sixteen. When he saw these girls, he said, "Patty, they look under age, are they legal?"

In 1982, I was booked into the Moulin Rouge in Vienna. It was a truly magnificent expansive theatre in the round, with red carpet and orchestra, modeled after the more famous namesake theatre in Paris, but on a much grander scale. It was massive in size, in terms of both diameter and height.

Moulin Rouge Vienna at Night

I was brought in as the lead dancer in a new show as a specialty act. I wore a sequined black velvet spider costume created by world famous designer, Hedy Jo Star, who had also designed the elaborate costumes for the Lido, Stardust, Jubilee, and Folies Bergere in Las Vegas.

Grandeur of the Moulin Rouge Vienna

I travelled with my beloved black and grey cat, Susan B Anthony, to Vienna and all over Europe. I named her after the famous women's rights activist who had just appeared on the new one dollar silver coin. In case she wandered off and got lost, Susie wore a yellow leather harness with a little snap wallet attached. Inside was a note and a hundred dollar bill. Of course, the money was eventually stolen. The note read, "I am Susan B Anthony. Please return me to my hotel."

I always stayed in hotels mainly because I liked the room service, and I could also get a massage, my hair done, and basically anything I needed. Although I always had a home base, my real home was on the road inside of a suitcase. To this day, I always prefer to drink my coffee out of a paper cup rather than a ceramic mug.

Susie was a one person cat and would only allow me to touch her. She would hiss and growl merely at the sight of my husband, Lew Warren, who would complain, "I hate that cat!" He may not have been fond of cats, but he was in love with expensive European cars, but he never took care of them, and they soon lost most of their value.

I Love Fluffy Hats and Fluffy Dogs

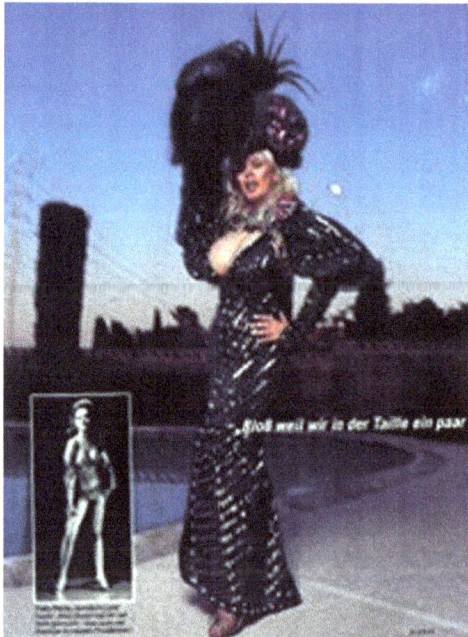

and Fancy Parisian Hats

and Stylish Hats

and Broad Brim Hats

I Love Light Blue Hats and Fast Red Cars

What Happens in Vegas

AFTER WORKING IN Hollywood, I returned to Vegas, where I reached a high level of fame in the late 70's and early 80's as a headline singer and dancer. Not only did my success bring financial rewards and plenty of publicity in the society columns, but I had the opportunity to live and work with some of the biggest stars and high rollers in Las Vegas.

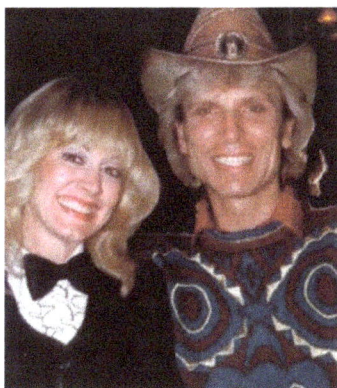

Iconic White Tiger Trainer Siegfried

THE OUTRAGEOUS
PATTY WRIGHT —
The best looking
showgirl in Las Vegas
is currently featured in
the fantastic production
by Steve Rossi
"Burlesque '79" at the
Holiday International
(Downtown). Rossi
gives it all to
showgoers in his
revue; showgirls, dan-
cing dolls, variety acts,
and the superb Joe
Bruno Orchestra.
Showtimes are 9 p.m.
& 11:30 p.m. no ad-
mission.

2C LAS VEGAS SUN   Sunday, June 17, 1979

R.S.V.P.
Marguerite Rittendale

Wright On
Harry Kukrin, general manager at the Holiday
International, gets the "Thatsa' Nice" award. When
Patty Wright of the Holiday Burlesque Show had her
parents Glenn and Connie Koester in from Wichita,
Kukrin changed the marquee early so that Patty's
parents could ogle her name in lights. Dad's comment
on the neon blockbuster, "All of those years of dance
lessons have finally paid off." After the elation died
out, Patty's real estate tycoon hubby Jack Hunt
propped dad in his pressurized Aeorstar and flew him
back to Kansas, where he's vice president of the Kansas
Gas and Electric Company.

THE WRIGHT WAY —
Patty Wright is stun-
ning the audiences in
"Burlesque '79" at the
Holiday International,
downtown.
Las Vegas MIRROR July 6, 1979

Gossip Column in Las Vegas Sun

Vegas Regular, Comedian David Brenner

Staying Cool

Rock Star Alice Cooper

Frankie Valli of the Four Seasons

I have known Steve Rossi so long that I can't remember how we first met. I appeared with him in one show after another during the pinnacle of my career in Vegas. Steve is probably best known for his comedy routine with Marty Allen, but their relationship had hit a sour note and for a number of years they were not on speaking terms. For a short time, Steve even lived at our home in Las Vegas. My husband Jack Hunt really liked Steve and thought that he was a great guy, but never adjusted to his over the top show business personality which he considered abnormal. For example, Steve would often tap on our bedroom door asking if we were still awake, and then without waiting for us to answer, just walk into our room while we were in bed. He would brazenly sit on the edge of our bed and start a conversation. Jack considered this behavior to be completely unacceptable and complained, "Your show business friends are killing me!"

Steve had entered show business at an early age having been discovered by none other than Mae West. She insisted that he shorten his real name, Joseph Charles Tafarella, to Steve Rossi, so that his long name would not overshadow hers on the marquee. They first appeared together in a comedy routine at Ciro's nightclub in LA, and later performed at the Sahara in Vegas. Steve was also a talented singer, and in the early 50's, he performed with a group called the Robinaires. In 1957, he formed the Allen & Rossi comedy duo, which was enormously successful in the late 50's and 60's, and they frequently appeared on the Ed Sullivan show. They reunited from time to time throughout the next three decades.

In 2001, he appeared with Brad Pitt in *The Mexican* appropriately playing a Vegas MC, and was also inducted into the "Show Business Legends Hall of Fame" at the Sahara that same year. Recently he has written a book with a ridiculously long title called *Adult Stand-up Comedy for Wannabe Comedians:*

Hilarious Stand-up Routines, Jokes and Stories, and appeared in an off Broadway play, *Don't Leave It All to Your Children* with actor and comedian, Ronnie Schell.

I first worked with Steve at the Treasury Hotel on the Strip next to the Tropicana in a show called *Topsy Turvy.* I replaced Tempest Storm as the headliner there when the mob sold the casino to Herb Pastor, an important figure in early Las Vegas history, who owned and operated several downtown casinos and strip joints. I was incredibly busy performing three shows in the afternoon and then three shows at night, as well as working on the choreography.

My most successful collaboration with Steve was as his co-star in an extravaganza called *Burlesque 79*, a reenactment of old Burlesque at the Holiday International Casino on the current downtown site of the Union Station Casino. Steve would perform as the headline singer and Master of Ceremonies, and I would dance in a routine called the "Bird of Paradise" wearing an elaborate plumed costume. The show was unique in that admission was free, and the audience was offered a complimentary buffet as well. This was an era when cheap buffets were the star attraction and the only thing that got bigger billing than Tony Martin or Patty Wright was Free Buffet, and we often joked about it. The show offered a full ensemble of showgirls and musicians and included acts by singer Debbie Goldman and juggler Wayne Mortensen.

We even added a comedy routine that was a satire on women using the lyrics to " I Am Going to Hate Myself in the Morning," but it never got off the ground.

Steve Rossi and Patty Wright in Burlesque '79

Burlesque '79 Marquee

Posing Nude in Las Vegas 1980

Another Vegas entertainer with whom I had a long relationship was Phyllis McGuire. She was discovered by Arthur
Godfrey and was a frequent quest on his TV show throughout
the 50's as the lead singer in the trio of McGuire Sisters. Her rise
to fame was so meteoric from obscure church choir to national
stardom that she had to see a psychiatrist, and she earned so

much cash that she could afford to wear custom made Channel suits worth fifteen grand apiece.

She is also somewhat notorious for her romantic relationship with Chicago gangster Sam Giancana, and even appeared as a witness in a Grand Jury investigation. She also managed to get involved with Bob Stupak and myself in a ménage a trois. When Bob broke his promise to take us along with him on a trip to Russia, we both refused to talk to him and this arrangement took a six-month respite.

I first met Neil Sedaka through his producer Jay Harvey at the Sands. Neil was an incredibly sweet guy and kind enough to let my daughter Glennel play piano on stage before his opening of his show.

Patty and Neil Sedaka with Jay Harvey's Aunt and Mother

Patty and Neil

I never met Mr. Las Vegas, Wayne Newton, but in contrast to his public image as clean cut and all American, he had a reputation with his fellow entertainers as a show off and playboy. Several of my girlfriends who had dated him would attest to his bad boy personality.

The very talented singer Tom Jones appeared on stage as the macho man who wore a sock in his pants to enhance his manhood making all of the ladies swoon. However, when I visited his home, he behaved more like a pussycat by catering to his wife's every whim.

I was introduced to Liberace by Steve Rossi on a Sunday afternoon at Bertha's Design Center where I bought all of my furniture. He was casually dressed in Jesus thongs and cut off jeans. He exclaimed, "Patty, it is so nice to meet you! Don't you like all of my rings? Do you like the way I dress? It is so freaking hot outside, isn't it!" I was delighted to meet him since I had been his number one fan ever since I caught his show at the Hilton Continental on Paradise along with my husband Jack Hunt.

I had a picture taken on stage with Georgie Jessel at the Landmark Hotel in Las Vegas, which is no longer standing. It was located on the corner of Paradise Road and Convention Center Dr. He called me up on stage that night and introduced me as his fiance. It was shot LIVE on stage. It was his very last performance ever! He went back to Israel and died about a week later!

Georgie Jessel in his Last Stage Appearance

I was even familiar to some extent with members of the legendary Rat Pack comprised of Frank Sinatra, Dean Martin, Sammy Davis Jr., Peter Lawford, and Joey Bishop. Almost all of their appearances at the Sands were sold out, and legions of their fans would pour into Las Vegas for a chance to see their show. The term Rat Pack was first applied to some well-known friends of Humphrey Bogart, and coined by journalists who referred to Bogie's home in LA, where the group regularly hung out, as the "Holmby Hills Rat Pack." Since Sinatra was a member of this original fraternity, the term was transferred with him to Las Vegas and applied to this new 60's group of performers.

Patty Joins the Rat Pack in a Game of Pool

I was lucky enough to meet Frank at Caesar's Palace when he yelled out Stevie across the room as a greeting to Rossi and I was then introduced to him.

Joey Bishop lived near my home on Spencer Street behind the Boulevard Mall and I would often see him drive his brand-new Rolls Royce Silver Shadow up and down the block.

I never met Sammy Davis, Jr. but I did have the opportunity to enjoy his show. I received an autographed copy of Sammy's life story, *Yes, I Can* from the author, Burt Boyar. A film version will finally be released in 2018 by Paramount Pictures. I had the good fortune to meet him on a flight to LA. Burt has also written two other best sellers on Sammy, an acclaimed book on the International Tennis Tour, and a controversial but well reviewed book titled, *How Franco Stopped Hitler*.

My most celebrated and long term relationship was with casino mogul, Bob Stupak, the "Polish Maverick." He also had political ambitions and mounted an unsuccessful campaign for Mayor of Las Vegas in 1986. Although he received constant attention from the press, he is probably best remembered as the owner and operator of Vegas World and the Stratosphere.

Vegas World was situated halfway between the Strip and downtown, and since it had an out of the way location, Bob needed a way to attract customers. The interior was unconventional with a replica of a spaceship and astronaut dangling from the ceiling, and a large plastic container supposedly filled with a million dollars in cash and casino chips. Oddball sucker games with unfavorable rules, like blackjack with both dealer cards exposed and crapless craps, replaced standard versions offered at other casinos. Although these variations appeared to give the player an added advantage, they actually increased the house percentage considerably. Slot machines offered automobiles as jackpots and gamblers could even bet against a caged chicken.

So Big Burlesque Marquee

Vacation packages that greatly inflated their actual value were offered to lure in large numbers of unsuspecting tourists. The promotional brochure explained it this way - the casino management expected to lose money on almost every vacation package but hoped to recover its losses from the few high rollers that could be brought into the casino. In 1991, Bob was fined $125,000 by the Nevada Gaming Commission for misleading the public. In 1992, Galaxy Theatre showcased So Big Burlesque, a tribute to old burlesque, with the legendary Steve Rossi and Marty Allen, Tony Martin, and Memories of Elvis.

The Stratosphere, which replaced Vegas World on the same site, boasted an 1189' tower with a restaurant, wedding chapel, and rollercoaster on the observation deck at the top. When it finally opened in 1996, it became an instant sensation with the tourists and permanently changed the Las Vegas skyline.

Bob was also an exceptional poker player and sports bettor, winning both the High-Low Poker competition in the World Series of Poker and a million dollar bet on the Super Bowl. For a time, it appeared that everything he touched turned to gold.

Bob Stupak at the Poker Table

However, his early life had been a struggle. He dropped out of high school becoming a teenage loan shark and motorcycle racer. His ability for self-promotion resulted in a contract with United Artists as a pop singer in the 50's using the name Bobby Star. Although he appeared in nightclubs and even recorded a Christmas song, his career as a singer never took off. On the advice of his father, who had operated a gambling racket in Pittsburg, he began selling coupon books to local restaurants and later moved his operation to Australia.

He eventually settled in Las Vegas where he first operated a restaurant, the Chateau Vegas, but failed to make a profit, and then a small casino named the Million Dollar Historic Gambling Museum, which burned down in less than two months. Since he had not followed fire codes, his insurance company refused at first to pay for the damages, but they eventually settled the claim for $300,000. Using this infusion of cash, Bob went on to operate the Glitter Gulch casino on Fremont Street, best known for displaying the iconic cowgirl, Vegas Vicky, in neon.

Bob was well aware of my friendship with Steve Rossi, and had such a secret crush on me that he paid Steve a cool ten grand just to arrange a meeting. Unfortunately, Steve just kept the money and never introduced us.

I finally did meet Bob at the Las Vegas Country Club through my boyfriend and future husband Michael Flores, who was his property manager. Bob was very good looking as well as goofy and eccentric. He would often accompany us over to Sam's Club where we would eat, drink, and gamble all night long winning or losing five or six grand, while laughing and raising hell.

I soon established a business relationship with Bob. I first worked for him in a show called *Body Heat,* a short run lounge act that seated about a hundred people. Lounge acts would open and close in Vegas hotels in a blink of the eye. I did not have much clout with him since I could be fired any time if I requested health insurance or a food allowance. Casino owners did not have any qualms about using their power to dominate and intimidate their employees, and job security did not exist in Vegas for most of the entertainers.

However, my situation improved considerably when I was offered a job as the headline singer and dancer at Vegas World. At the time, I was receiving a generous allowance from my husband Lew Warren, and enjoying daily trips to the ski slopes, so I was in a strong position to negotiate. I accepted the job after Bob made a generous offer of $5000 a week for only one show a night. I also received a number of perks including health insurance, a food allowance, and free access to anything in the hotel.

I performed in a well-choreographed and highly erotic routine. I was given a dramatic introduction – "You may have seen her on TV, in magazines, and in Playboy. Here she is, the voluptuous Patty Plenty." I then appeared on stage wearing a low cut sparkling blue evening gown, with a large pink boa wrapped around my shoulders, moving sensuously to the romantic sounds and lyrics of "Amor, Amor, Amor," by Julio Iglesias. When this first song ended, I somehow managed to quickly remove the gown without losing a step, exposing a sparkling blue teddy, well toned legs and buttocks, and even more cleavage. In the final stage of my routine, I received howls from the audience as I removed the teddy exposing all of my assets, wearing only a G-string. However, I carried two large pink plumes which I used to strategically and rhythmically cover what I had just exposed. In my final pose, I held out the plumes at arms length to the cheers and whistles of the audience.

Although Bob was closely involved with the show, we avoided a more personal relationship until I filed for a divorce from Lew. I called Bob to inform him that I was getting a divorce and he invited me to Café Michelle for a drink. We were so hounded by locals, who recognized us and begged for our autographs, that we had to retreat to Caesar's Palace. We were such well known celebrities in Vegas that nobody would ever leave us alone.

We began a romantic relationship that lasted from 1992 until his death in 2009. Bob was extremely generous and on several of our dates, he would just hand over ten grand with no strings attached. One of our favorite activities was to spend all day at the movies gorging ourselves on popcorn.

I quickly became friends with his son, Nevada, and his two daughters, Summer and Nicole. I watched them grow up, and remain on excellent terms with them to this day.

We were never married although he did propose to me on several occasions. Since I found him to be very difficult to get along with, I would always decline. He tried to gain additional publicity from our relationship by informing the press that we were planning to go on a cruise to Alaska, and he would use the opportunity to propose to me.

Our normal routine was to stay out all night, drinking and gambling until day break. I became exhausted after several months of this, and I just couldn't stand it anymore. I pleaded, "Bob, I am so fucking bored that I just want to go home and go to bed. Can't I just take the limo back to your place and when you get home, I should still be there – maybe!"

Our relationship cooled to absolute zero when he promised to pay me $200 a day just for staying away from him altogether. I would show up every day at the cashier's cage at the

Stratosphere to collect my money. This arrangement went on for several months, but he eventually started to miss me. This time he went to the other extreme and agreed to pay me $1000 a minute just to keep him company for fifteen minutes.

In 1995, Bob was severely injured in a terrible motorcycle accident, hitting the pavement face first, losing several teeth, shattering facial bones, and even damaging a portion of his brain. I first learned about the accident from Bob's producer, Jay Harvey, who told me, "Patty, Bob has been in a terrible accident." I didn't believe it at first because Jay was always jealous of Bob so I replied, "Yeah right, it's April Fool's Day." Jay answered, "No Patty, it's not April Fool's Day. It really did happen." When I learned that it actually was true, I went bezerk, and only then did I realize how much I loved him.

Bob remained in a coma for several months. He was kept alive because the hospital didn't want to have his death on their record, and somehow he miraculously recovered. He had been brilliant when he operated Vegas World and the Stratosphere, but he became only a shadow of himself, and even more impossible to get along with. He readily admitted, "I am not the man I used to be!"

In recent years, Bob would visit me in Hawaii, staying at upscale hotels in Kahala, just east of Waikiki. He really enjoyed the Hawaiian lifestyle but never developed a taste for Hawaiian music, preferring old standards by Sinatra. However, our relationship remained unsettled since he became much more conservative in doling out his still sizeable fortune, refusing to upgrade my beach house on the North Shore.

I was deeply saddened by his death in September 2009, and become very emotional whenever I remember him.

My relationship with Jay Harvey definitely started out on the wrong foot. Jay had been hired by Bob because he had experience working for the William Morris Agency, and the current show, *So Big Burlesque,* was in trouble, although it had been quite successful for a number of years. One of the routines was a reenactment of an old burlesque classic, "The Transformer." I played the part of a sexy nurse who collaborated with a lecherous quack. Patients who suffered from various medical problems would be connected to a machine that somehow transferred their conditions to a dummy. However, I had forgotten to order a dummy, but was able to convince my unsuspecting dimwitted boyfriend to substitute for one. The first patient was a gorgeous young woman who the doctor was able to entice into his office by curing her of itching, and a second young woman was cured of stammering. My unfortunate boyfriend inherited both of these symptoms. The third patient was a gay man who wanted to be straight, and some very offensive jokes were tossed around. The final patient was a pregnant woman. My boyfriend wasn't going to inherit that condition, and quickly headed for the exits. Obviously, the age of burlesque was ready to be put to rest.

Since Bob was madly in love with me and couldn't bear to give me the bad news in person, he had Jay inform me that my salary would be reduced from $5000 to $2000 a week because the show was losing money. Obviously, this did not go over well with me and I erupted into a tantrum shouting out, "What the fuck are you talking about? Do you know who you are talking to, young man?" He replied, "I think I am talking to Patty Plenty." I exclaimed, " You're damn right! Does Bob know you are here?" Jay asserted, "Bob hired me!" I angrily replied, "I don't believe you, you mother fucker!"

The news got even worse when Jay went on to say that unless there was a big change, the show would close within six weeks and that I should tell all of my little friends in the show to start saving their money. The cast already hated me because they were only being paid a paltry $300 a week.

To make matters still worse, a bottle of Dom Perignon and a big bouquet of flowers with a note from Bob would arrive at my dressing room before every show. However, I had made the arrangements myself and this was just a ruse to reinforce my celebrity status. The other performers would exclaim, "Oh, not again!" and I would reply in a sarcastic voice,"I can't help it if Bob loves me, and he doesn't love you guys." Nobody ever got wind of this scheme and it only made me even more unpopular, if that was even possible.

Despite the initial bad blood between us, I eventually began quite good friends with Jay. He had made a reputation for himself in LA as the youngest producer in the history of Hollywood. He had arrived in Vegas temporarily to book a show for comedian, Sam Kinnison, but unfortunately Sam went to Tahoe to get married and was killed in an automobile accident.

Jay told me, "Patty, something tells me that I should pack up all of my furniture and head back to Hollywood, However, I am a smart man and I made millions in Hollywood, so Vegas will be a cinch."

He was soon hired to produce most of the big shows at the major casinos including those for Tom Jones and Madonna. However, he just didn't fit into the Las Vegas culture, and against my advice, he was openly critical of the casino managers, who all had enormous egos. Despite his demonstrated talent, he soon found himself out of a job at all of the casinos.

Recently, I had the opportunity to reunite with Steve Rossi when he returned to Vegas to host a comedy show of talented new comedians at LVH, the former Las Vegas Hilton, and currently the Westgate. I impulsively decided to call him up, and he graciously invited me to the show. He had just undergone heart surgery but still appeared to be in good spirits. We talked about old times, and I saw that he had not lost his old form as he did an impromptu stand up routine at the beginning of the show.

Steve also helped produce another show at the new Hilton starring versatile impressionist, Rich Little, who played the part of Jimmy Stewart reminiscing over his long career. The show provided Steve with badly needed income. This format gave Rich the opportunity to impersonate many of the legendary celebrities of prior decades like Humphrey Bogart and Walter Brennan. Steve helped to modernize the show by adding comedy lines related to recent events. One of Rich's best impressions was that of Johnny Carson in the classic role of Karnak. He held a sealed envelope to his temple as he foretold the answer to the secret question, "clapitty clap, bang bang, clappity clap, clappity clap, bang bang, clappity clap, bang bang, bang bang." As the audience made a miserable attempt to repeat, Karnak chided "Oh, shut up!" He then opened the envelope to reveal the hilarious hidden question, "Describe an Amish drive-by shooting."

The show ended on a surprising note as Rich approached the audience to ask if they recognized most of the impressions, and whether he should take the show to Broadway.

After the show, Steve and I, along with a couple of friends, decided to watch his son Dino perform in a band at the M resort located well south of the Strip. I volunteered to drive my friend's red Mustang, but unfortunately, I was not up to the task. Since I was quite drunk, I couldn't locate the headlights, and made an uncoordinated attempt to move the car forward, resulting in a violent herky jerky motion. Steve, who had just had a pacemaker installed, begged for mercy and demanded a new driver, as he was tossed back and forth in his seat. On the way to the resort, I learned the fate of some of our former celebrity friends, many of whom, like Tony Martin, had recently passed away.

About a month later, I received a call from ex-husband Michael Flores who told me that he was very concerned that Steve's health was deteriorating since he had lost a large amount of weight and was not eating. I called Steve to tell him that I loved him and missed him, but he never returned my call. Unfortunately, he was diagnosed with fourth stage cancer that had progressively spread throughout his body, and could not be saved. I never visited him at the hospital because I just could not bear to see him dying.

His funeral was held in Las Vegas at a church near the Mercedes dealership on Sahara. It was a grand event attended by an impressive array of show business friends accumulated over the decades, including his long time comedy partner, Marty Allen, who was still kicking at the age of 92. It was a big media circus attended by at least 500, most of whom were in show business, along with a few wannabes who just wanted to be noticed. It was a celebration of his life and there were numerous eulogies attesting to his great achievements and character. Rich Little gave an impressive eulogy full of both emotion and humor. Steve would have been very pleased with this overwhelming show of affection. It was evident that he was universally loved by everyone who had known him.

I had the opportunity to meet with old friends and acquaintances. Michael, appearing tired, walked down the aisle to tell me that Jay Harvey was sitting up front. I asked Michael, "Should I go talk to him?" and he replied, "Well, I wouldn't." Michael was still angry at Jay because he had borrowed a hundred bucks to play a round of golf but never paid him back. As Michael kept on walking past me, I jumped out of my seat and ran up the aisle. I extended my hand and exclaimed, "Jay, it is so good to see you. I am so sorry that it has to be here." Recovering from shock, he managed to utter a weak "Oh, Oh Hi." He explained that he had come to Vegas just for the funeral, and I told him that I had come all the way from Hawaii. We then engaged in some small talk as he remained seated in the church pew, and I had to squat down to his level in order to hear him. We had a lot to talk about since we once had a five year romantic relationship while living in separate houses on the Las Vegas Country Club. I would stay at his place for most of the week and only occasionally return to my place. He preferred not to stay at my house because he didn't think that it was appropriate. He eventually returned to Beverly Hills and I followed him there. He asked me to marry him, but I refused since he was too much of a gambler, and I needed to have a more stable partner. I loved him but I just didn't think he was marriage material.

Patty and Producer Jay Harvey

Halloween in Vegas

While on my frequent trips to Vegas, I often go to the Pamplemousse, a popular landmark restaurant on Sahara just east of Paradise. The restaurant's name, which means "grapefruit" in French, was recommended to owner Georges LaForge by late singer Bobby Darin. It offers a fantastic five course meal starting with a healthy basket of crisp fresh vegetables, soup, sorbet in champagne, a main course of steak or fish, and ending with a dessert. The décor is magnificent evoking a cozy French inn.

On a recent visit, I and my friend Norman met an interesting couple from San Diego and we decided to share a table. We quickly became such close friends that I actually exchanged topless pictures with the other gorgeous blond. We were making such a racket that a big nasty man approached us to complain that we were ruining his dinner. We laughed it off and continued to have fun with our waiter Keifer, who liked to perform silly song and dance routines for us.

George LaForge, Owner of Pamplemousse

I often go to another classic restaurant, Piero's, with my good friend Flo, who lives at the nearby Las Vegas Country Club. It has been a legendary Vegas night spot on Convention Center Drive for more than thirty years, and the meeting place to dine and drink for casino executives, mobsters, politicians, and entertainers. They come for the cuisine, for the secluded dining areas. and the attentive but discreet staff. The owner is Freddie Glusman, who has befriended and served all of the movers and shakers in Las Vegas for over thirty years. You can often hear his loud raspy voice rise above the background noise as he greets his customers and directs his veteran staff. This place exudes the past. You can imagine seeing Sammy

Davis, Dean Martin, and Frank Sinatra sitting in the plush high-back chairs after a Rat Pack performance across the room from such underworld figures as Fat Herbie Blitzstein and Tony The Ant Spilotro, who once crushed a fellow gangster's head in a vice until his eyes popped out. You could imagine that the FBI was still occupying space across the street to spy on these notorious mob figures. It was even the setting for the restaurant scenes in the classic Vegas movie, *Casino*. Las Vegas locals enjoy such signature Italian dishes as osso buco and scaloppini Milanese. The menu is not only varied and but offers daily specials. On any given day, patrons of Piero's could see such celebrities as Jerry Lewis, Nicholas Cage, and Rich Little along with national sports figures like Michael Jordan, Magic Johnson, and Shaquille O'Neal.

In fact, I was invited by Freddie to a Super Bowl party to watch the Patriots pull out a last second win against the Seahawks. We were served an assortment of appetizers including pastrami on rye, gourmet meatballs, pickles, and barbeque spare ribs. I spotted Steve Lawrence who looked incredible for his age, and we recorded the event with a selfie.

On Friday and Saturday nights, you could hear diminutive singer Pia Zadora, who had reserved a corner of the restaurant called Pia's Place, combine with legendary Sinatra pianist, Vincent Falcone, to render versions of Sinatra standards and oher timeless classics.

Pia Zadora at Piero's

Singer Steve Lawrence with Patty at Piero's

Patty and Flo Celebrating New Year's Eve 2018 at Piero's

The Seven Dwarfs or the Magnificent Seven?

EVEN BY HOLLYWOOD standards, I've been married an astonishing number of times. However, to put it in perspective, I still need one more husband to match the late beloved actress, Elizabeth Taylor, and two more to catch up to recently deceased Zsa Zsa Gabor, who has tied the knot an incredible nine times. We all remember former New York governor Elliot Spitzer as number nine but that is another story. None of my husbands ever attained the fame of an Eddie Fisher, a Richard Burton, or even a Conrad Hilton. Nor did they gain the level of notoriety of Prince Frederic von Anhalt, Zsa Zsa's last mate, who claimed that he was the father of Anna Nicole Smith's daughter. Nevertheless, for the most part, they were quite successful in their chosen careers

and very wealthy. One could even say that each new hubby provided me with both a larger house and a bigger bustline.

In the classic 1960 film, *The Magnificent Seven*, a small
group of seven hired guns defends a remote Mexican village
from a horde of a hundred banditos. In one dramatic scene,
the leader of the American gunslingers played by Yul Bryner is
confronted by the leader of the Mexican outlaws played by Eli
Wallach who taunts, "You don't have many men." In a defiant
and menacing tone, Bryner replies, "I have ENOUGH!" I would
certainly have to agree that SEVEN MEN IS ENOUGH!

To my first husband, Tom Wright, I owe the stage name that
I used in my early career, Patty Wright, but not much more. He
was the cute and talented drummer in a local Wichita band
who preferred Rock and Roll but was forced to play mostly
Country and Western to earn a living. When we first met, I was
only eighteen and he was a couple of years older. We were very
much in love and we decided to marry a year later. Eventually,
my dancing career started to take off when I flew to Hollywood
to take on the role of a go-go dancer in my first movie, The
Gypsy Moths. In contrast, his career never got off the ground as
he displayed little ambition. He was physically well endowed
but unfortunately this trait did not extend to above the belt. I
began to realize that he was turning into a loser and that he
needed to change. When he refused to give up smoking pot, I

decided that it was time to move on. Surprisingly, he was quite indifferent to our breakup, while I was devastated.

Another year went by before I met my next husband, John Henry. At the time he was married to a wealthy girl named Theresa Connolly whose family had made their fortune in the Wichita lumber business. He was a very handsome stockbroker of Lebanese descent who in fact resembled a young Danny Thomas, but for some reason told everyone that he was Syrian. Unlike his legendary namesake who was a steel driving man, this John Henry was more of a deal driving man.

He made a considerable income buying and selling over the counter stocks at a time when brokers had a monopoly on trading long before internet accounts like Ameritrade and Scottrade became available to the general public. However, his income would fluctuate wildly since he could win or lose as much as forty thousand in a single day. Whenever he had a good day, he was very generous indeed buying me expensive dresses. Unfortunately, on a bad day, he would ask me to return everything. Of course, this did not sit very well with me.

He was painfully aware of his social status being quite uncomfortable with my career as a stripper. However, he was more than willing to accept the considerable income I was making on the road which usually exceeded his own earnings. When I finally decided to divorce him, I called his former wife, Theresa, to let her know that I should have heeded her warning that he was no good. She was excited to hear from me and we became close friends, if you know what I mean.

Second Husband John Henry

My third husband, George Etherington, was considerably older than me, having been born in 1921, resulting in an age disparity of twenty-seven years. He was the actual nephew of Dwight D Eisenhower and displayed a photograph of himself shaking hands with his famous uncle while serving as an infantry soldier in Europe during World War II. He was very small in stature but had an ego that was larger than life.

I met George in the capital city of Topeka where I was earning my GRI, an important commercial real estate certification, while my dancing career was on hold. Since we attended the same classes, George would constantly flirt with me and ask me out. At the time, I had a serious relationship with real estate developer and future husband, Jack Hunt, who was annoyed with George's advances derisively calling him Georgie Porgie. However, George was not to be denied. When George told me, "I am real real rich," I replied "so is my boyfriend." When he said, "I have a fancy car," I replied "so does my boyfriend." When he said, "I am going to spend millions of dollars on you and I think I love you," I continued with my mantra "so does my boyfriend." Not one to give up easily, he pleaded "I just want you to go out to dinner with me." Admiring his persistence, I finally agreed. Besides, I always like to keep one on deck in case the batter strikes out. On the big night of our first date, George proudly drove up in a brand new Rolls Royce Silver Shadow. I teased him by joking that this was the just the kind of car that an old man would drive.

I quickly became quite fond of George since he was extremely generous and would do anything to please me. In fact, he proved to be the most generous of all of my husbands. He was also very eccentric and unpredictable. One night, we went to see Foster Brooks, the comedian who played the loveable lush. On the spur of the moment, George asked me if I would like to have Foster Brook's autograph. Being an outstanding athlete, he proceeded to jump over the table and run up the aisle pursuing a terrified Foster Brooks asking him to sign an autograph for Patty. While we were dating, he probably spent at least five hundred grand on gifts calling them little doodles and babbles. He even special ordered a Lincoln Mark IV in my favorite color pink even though I already had a new car. When the car failed to arrive on time for my birthday, George felt terrible about the situation and proceeded to buy a hundred shares of stock in my favorite company, Kansas Gas and Electric, where my father was Vice President, to help ease my anxiety.

I finally decided to marry him when he agreed to buy a new home in Las Vegas, all of the furniture, and even more fancy cars. The morning after our wedding, I received the shock of my life when he woke up and exclaimed, "Boy, when I get around to it, I will file for my divorce." In a stunned voice, I blurted out, "You are going to do what! You are going to do what!" I had just married a bigamist! As I proceeded to call the District Attorney, George made a run for it but he was eventually picked up at Caesar's Palace in the early morning wearing an expensive white three piece suit and sporting the hat of a Mississippi Riverboat gambler.

After the Georgie Porgie fiasco, I resumed my relationship with Jack Hunt, who interestingly enough, was born the same year as George. He had something else in common with George – he was a combat veteran in World War II. He fought both in Italy where he earned a Purple Heart and in Germany where he helped liberate the concentration camp at Dachau near Munich. He even received a commission as an Army Captain. While in Italy, he would send some Italian lire back home to his wife who, not realizing its value, unwittingly threw it away.

He grew up in an orphanage and borrowed the name Hunt from a local fireman, Dick Hunt, whom he admired as a child. Jack acquired an interest in building and developing while serving in the Civilian Conservation Corps during the Great Depression.

I first met Jack at age twenty while I was dancing in a night-club that he owned. He had rugged good looks with a lock of prematurely grey hair. We exchanged glances and it was love at first sight. At the time, he was a widower having lost his wife in a terrible accident a year earlier. She had been killed when a motorcycle slammed into her while on vacation in Laguna Beach. Jack survived but was injured when the cycle ran over his toes.

George may have been the most generous of my husbands, but Jack was easily my favorite. He was always positive, always fun, and always supportive. In addition, he continually helped me to improve myself. It was Jack who insisted that I enroll in the GRI commercial real estate course in Topeka.

During our first year of dating, we flew around in his private plane more that we drove in his fancy cars. He was an excellent pilot and I learned a lot from just watching him maneuver the plane. Often, he would allow me to take over the controls myself and I must have flown over a hundred hours under his guidance. He even insisted that I earn a pilot's license in case he suddenly became incapacitated. I soon embarked on a difficult training regimen. Even after six months of ground instruction and thirteen hours of solo time, I was not ready for my next task – to land the plane on my own. I was amazed by the amount of coordination and corrective action that was required. An amateur pilot would have little or no chance to make a safe landing despite the stories we have heard about some passenger heroically taking over the controls from a dead pilot. Several of our friends actually did crash and burn.

We traveled extensively all over the world. On one occasion, I booked a show in Guam without telling him. Even though he was quite upset, he decided to join me during my last week there. We spent a considerable amount of time learning to scuba dive. From the shoreline, we could see the outline of shipwrecks from the Spanish American War and World War II. However, the view was far more spectacular when we plunged sixty feet beneath the waves to get a closer look. We extended our trip spending a week in the Phillippines, a week in Hong Kong and Macao, a week in Japan, and a week in Hawaii before we finally returned to our home in Las Vegas. We owned several other homes including one in Wichita.

On another occasion, we travelled to Surinam, formerly Dutch Guiana, a small country in South America north of Brazil. We are all familiar with Devil's Island in neighboring French Guiana from the movie, *Papillon*, and this place was just as remote and forbidding. We were warned by the country's Bureau of Tourism not to put our hands into the muddy river water to avoid losing our fingers to the flesh-eating piranha.

We dated for four and half years and I was growing impatient. I was only going to give him another six months to pop the question or I would dump him. The words that he chose for his proposal reflected his well known sense of humor, "Patty, against my better judgment, will you marry me?"

Jack and Patty on their Wedding Night

I have always loved expensive cars and no car ever surpassed the custom made Diamonte that Jack gave to me as a gift. It was built on a Cadillac chassis and designed to resemble the long and sleek Duesenberg, a classic car first built in 1928 driven by such Hollywood legends as Clark Gable and Mae West. The Diamonte, priced at a hefty one hundred fifty grand, was very rare and only twenty-seven had been built. Loni Anderson was one of the owners as well. A special feature that Jack requested was a diamond in the center of the glove box with the inscription, "Especially made for Jack and Patty Hunt."

My New Diamonte

He was a very successful real estate developer. He had actually done business with my father in the fifties but I only realized this several years later. Over the course of his career, he built a multitude of homes, apartments, shopping centers, nursing homes, mobile home parks, and other projects. He received several prestigious rewards including Realtor of the Year, Most Valuable Citizen, and the Lifetime Achievement Award. However, he never sought the limelight and would quietly counsel younger real estate brokers. He also supported conservative causes and was very committed to the growth and development of Wichita.

Our relationship had a good long run but I wanted my show business career to have a long run even more. Being a straight shooter, Jack never quite fit into the Hollywood lifestyle. Once when we were guests at Steve Rossi's beautiful home in Encino, he became very upset with the constant yelling and bickering between Steve and his wife, not unusual behavior for temperamental celebrity couples.

He needed the full time attention of a devoted wife and this led to our breakup. I had been his third wife, and two more were to follow. He asserted that he preferred younger women and could easily afford to have one. He was not averse to having cosmetic surgery in order to appear more youthful. The age disparity with each new wife kept increasing. He was forty-seven years older than his last wife, Vicki. They were married for fourteen years and were regulars at Western dance clubs on Friday nights.

We remained friends until his death at age 87 in July, 2008. I attended his funeral at Tranquility Farm, his very spacious home in Andover, Kansas. I was told by his friends that I had been his favorite wife - just as he had been my favorite husband.

My fifth husband, Michael Flores, was very self confident and not averse to taking risks. He grew up in Saginaw, Michigan working in the family auto painting business started by his father, but left home to pursue an acting career. He attended the Pasadena Playhouse College of Theatre Arts, an accredited drama school where many Hollywood celebrities learned their craft, that offered a variety of courses in acting and directing as well as in set building and design. While attending classes, he met Rebecca Welles, the daughter of Rita Hayworth and Orson Welles, with whom he was engaged to for a year. For about three years they lived with Rita Hayworth in her home on Hartford Way just behind the Beverly Hills Hotel. At the time, Rita was suffering from an advanced stage of Alzheimer's disease and displayed violent outbursts of temper. In addition, she had a terrible drinking problem consuming as much as a fifth of vodka every night.

At the age of 21, he moved to Las Vegas and ironically his first job was to deal 21. He met Eddie Torres in a coffee shop who referred him to the downtown Fremont casino where he started dealing live games after two weeks of practice. He eventually became manager of the Silver Nugget, a large casino in North Las Vegas owned by Major Riddle, a Las Vegas legend who also owned the Dunes. His actual first name was Major and he had made a fortune in both oil and trucking, but lost a good share of it as an incredibly inept poker player in some well publicized high stakes games. Michael was later to lose his gaming license for allegedly dealing in cocaine.

I met Michael for the first time while he was playing tennis with my good friend Steve Rossi at the Las Vegas Country Club. Michael financed a successful advertising business operated by Steve. All three of us drove a Mercedes 450SL, and along with Bob Stupak, owned nearby homes in this strategically located resort close to the Las Vegas Strip. The property was originally the site of the Las Vegas Downs. When this thoroughbred racetrack went bankrupt, it was converted into the Las Vegas International Country Club in 1967 and later became the Bonanza County Club and Corral and finally a private country club simply named the Las Vegas Country Club. Michael would go on to become President of the Master Homeowner's Association.

A funny incident that reveals my early relationship with both Michael and Bob revolved around a trip to the Bahamas for the George Foreman/Muhammad Ali fight that Bob planned for a group of his buddies. When Michael told me about the trip, I replied that I would love to go with him. When Michael explained that it was just for the guys and that Bob would never allow me to go, I became even more determined. I found out what flight they were taking, showed up wearing a cowgirl hat, a wig and a scarf, and took a seat a couple rows ahead of Michael. As soon as the flight took off, I took off my disguise and blurted out "Oh boy, are we going to have a real good time!" Stupak became enraged and started screaming, "Who the fuck invited her, God damn it, God damn it." Michael was taken completely by surprise and nervously looked down at the floor, and the flight attendants became unraveled. Bob insisted in no uncertain terms that Michael and I would just have to go somewhere else. Michael was not one to challenge Stupak, and we ended up spending the weekend in Curacao, a relatively unknown island in the Dutch Antilles, near the now infamous island of Aruba where Natalie Holloway was murdered.

Michael and I dated a year before we decided to get married. On the night of our wedding, we celebrated along with our parents at one of my favorite restaurants, the Chateau Vegas, a five star restaurant once owned by Bob. I was embarrassed when Michael's mother, who was quite a kidder, loudly exclaimed, "What kind of restaurant doesn't have mashed taters? Who picked this restaurant?" My mother was not amused and asserted that she had chosen this restaurant and not me.

This was not a good omen. My marriage to Michael quickly descended into open warfare. Although we were married, we maintained separate homes on opposite sides of a fairway inside the Las Vegas Country Club. One night, when I arrived at Michael's very expensive home, he failed to answer the intercom because he was in the spa located a short distance from the house. I became frustrated and started kicking the beautiful French doors that he had just painted. This definitely got his attention and he yelled, "What the fuck are you doing." When he finally arrived, he noticed that the doors had been badly scuffed. He turned me around by telling me to look over there and then kicked me in the ass while screaming "Don't ever kick these fucking doors again." I became enraged and swore at him. I then punched him in the gut, got into my 450SL and rammed it into his garage door dislodging it from its hinges, damaging both his Rolls Royce Silver Shadow and his Mercedes 450SL parked inside. I quickly returned to my condo on the other side of the fairway and retreated inside. A few minutes later, Michael arrived at my front door with a sledgehammer, and asked in a menacing tone, "Patty, Patty, are you busy? You will have to come back." He then took the sledgehammer and broke off the door handle. I was on the balcony behind some glass doors and in a falsetto voice pleaded, "Help, Help." He then replied," I will give you some help". He walked up to the balcony and proceeded to shatter the glass doors. I angrily replied, "I hope that you are happy now. Are you finished?" He said "Well, I don't know. Let me see". He noticed a big TV decorated with mirrors and with one mighty blow put a huge round hole into it, just missing my cat in the process. He then exclaimed, "Now I'm finished." As he made his exit, he was stopped by security who wrote him up for all the damage to my property. However, he let me off the hook for the damage I had done to his property by claiming that it had been an accident.

On another occasion, I arrived drunk at his home at six in the morning. I rang the intercom and asked Michael if he was going to let me in. He sarcastically replied "No". I rang it again and he again answered "No". I then warned, "If you don't let me in, I am going to take off all of my clothes and just stand here and here comes security". He replied "Go ahead and put on a show, do it real slow, take off one piece at a time, and I am sure you will get his attention." The security guard was startled to see me naked and asked Michael over the intercom what was going on. Michael explained, "That is my wife. She is a little dazed and confused. Did she take all of her clothes off? Are you looking at her breasts?" The guard replied "It's kind of hard not to notice." Michael finally agreed to let me inside but after I ascended the spiral staircase to the balcony, he refused to let me into the master bedroom. I became enraged, stormed out of the house, threw my expensive Louis Vuitton handbag into the pool, and proceeded to walk completely naked toward my home on the other side of the fairway.

Fifth Husband Michael Flores

As you probably have guessed, my marriage to Michael was not to endure - it lasted only a year and a half. The last straw was a dispute over twenty-five grand of "borrowed" money. I started divorce proceedings and tried to get my money back. Unfortunately the judge ruled against me stating that a husband could legally acquire any joint property from his wife. However, he was sympathetic to my case stating that if this were a court of morals, he would have to rule in my favor. He also rendered the opinion "Michael Flores would rather climb a tree and tell a lie than stand on the ground and tell the truth."

A few years ago, after losing a considerable amount of weight, Michael tried to get back with me by sending a photo of his new trim self, but needless to say, our relationship had more than just a weight problem. However, today, we have a relatively genial relationship and still communicate on a regular basis.

Although Michael had more than his share of legal problems, he operated a successful and legitimate real estate business. One of his many properties was the thirty-six unit Villa de Flores apartment complex just off of the Vegas Strip. In 1990, casino magnate Steve Wynn needed to buy the property to make way for his new luxury casino, the Mirage. These plain stucco two story apartments, besides being quite an eyesore, were located in the middle of an area that was designated to be a main parking lot for the upscale Mirage, an innovative complex in the center of the Strip with a tropical theme. After long months of negotiation, Steve made a fair offer of 3.7 million and actually cut a check for that amount.

When Wynn refused to cover additional costs and fees involved in the transaction, Michael refused to accept the check and a chapter in Las Vegas history was written. Michael was approached by Ralph Englestad, the owner of the Imperial Palace and a long time rival of Steve Wynn, who offered a bid of six million in order to inflate the value of the property. Englestad was a colorful character who had once been fined 1.5 million dollars by the Nevada Gaming Commission for wearing a Nazi uniform on Hitler's birthday.

The local press aggressively covered the story and a war of words between Steve and Michael ensued. Steve referred to Michael as the "schmuck with the apartments" and Michael countered by telling the press that "Steve Wynn was to the Good Neighbor policy what Jeffrey Dahmer was to dining etiquette." Steve then resorted to intimidation by deliberately placing three massive propane capsules directly in front of Michael's office. The tanks were used to fuel the fireworks and volcano eruption on the Strip and could have been placed anywhere on the seventeen acre property. Steve vehemently denied that this presented a hazard. However, on one occasion, the roof of the apartments actually caught on fire. A flurry of lawsuits then ensued between the two rivals. In spite of everything, Michael both literally and figuratively held his ground and Steve was forced to build massive parking garages around the apartments. To this day, the Villa de Flores stands defiant remaining quite literally a thorn in the side of Steve Wynn.

Michael had both a personal and business relationship with Bob Stupak for over thirty years. He managed all of Bob's properties including the Thunderbird Hotel, Vegas World and the Stratosphere, a truly unique casino located halfway between the strip and downtown, with an imposing 1149' tower.

After very challenging construction problems and even a fire, this innovative casino finally opened in April 1996 amid widespread acclaim. However, the project was not a financial success, and Bob Stupak lost almost all of his investment when the stock plummeted from $17 to a few cents in only a few months. Michael was also heavily invested in the project but managed to avoid serious losses. The only winner turned out to corporate raider, Carl Icahn, who purchased a major interest in the restructured project at a greatly reduced price.

Even by my own standards, my sixth marriage to Lynn Thomas was incredibly short – just two weeks! I sometimes even have a hard time remembering his name although he does, in some ways, stand out from the other husbands. To his credit, he successfully operated a PVC manufacturing company, despite having to deal with polio and walking on crutches.

Lynn quickly became suspicious of my every move. I would often get up in the middle of the night at 4 AM to buy donuts when the coffee shops opened. Sometimes I would stay out three or four hours at a time and this was more than he could tolerate. Possessing a jealous nature, he demanded to know where I had gone and his suspicious attitude quickly led to yet another divorce.

When it became time to divide up the property, Lynn forged an alliance with Michael Flores by offering him fifty grand to testify against me in court. This strategy had only limited success. Lynn was able to keep the house with the big mortgage and

I retained the other one that was already in my name. When I liquidated half of the furniture, one of the many items sold was his Lacy Boy recliner. However, I soon learned in court that this particular chair had been Lynn's prized possession. He literally cried and whined to the judge that he desperately wanted his Lazy Boy back. I glanced at my parents who had attended the proceedings, and we all agreed that Lynn was quite a loon.

My seventh and last husband, Lew Warren, was even more eccentric than the others and by far the most devious. He somewhat resembled both the comedian Danny Kaye and the dancer Donald O'Connor and always had a mischievous look on his face. He owned half of the depressed property in downtown Las Vegas, but if you asked his tenants, they would not describe him as a slum lord, but as a scum lord. Woe to anyone who happened to be a day late on their rent. He would seize furniture, TVs, VCRs, anything of value, store the items in some hidden away property, and then put the poor tenant out on the street. He would sell homes to people that he knew could not afford them. After they made three or four payments, but missed the next payment, they would face foreclosure.

Although he was raking in a fortune from his various properties, he would do almost anything to save small amounts of money. Even at age sixty, he would do roof repairs in the extreme heat of a Las Vegas summer just to save the seven dollars an hour that it would have cost to hire someone else. Lew was also a very talented entertainer performing as a stand up comic and MC, but primarily as a ventriloquist. Using the stage name of Lou DuPont, he performed an innovative routine in which he simultaneously sang with all three of his dummies. He even created some of the dummies used by famous ventriloquist Edgar Bergen, father of actress Candice Bergen.

**Ventriloquist Lou DuPont with
Sony, Kugel, and Tondalaya**

Lew with Brother and Actor Rayford Barnes

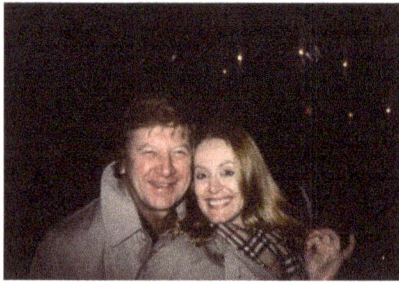

Lew and Patty in San Francisco

Celebrating My Birthday and Pregnancy

He displayed all of the traits of an incurable work-a-holic, waking up at 6 AM, working all day to 6 PM, performing his show in the evening, drinking vodka all night, and then after getting only two hours of sleep, starting the same routine all over again. On a positive note, I did obtain some valuable coaching from him to further my career. We had separate acts in the same show, and he would diligently work with me on my comedy routine, improving both the timing and the material. My good friend, Kitten Natividad, who also had a career in both mainstream and adult films, agrees that Lew had been an invaluable mentor during this stage of my life.

Another one of his talents was an amazing facility with languages, being fluent in six and familiar with another twelve. He would travel to some new country and in a few days learn enough of the native language to do a comedy routine entirely in that language. We peformed in most of the countries of Europe and the Middle East. He even performed with the USO in Vietnam for two years but ended that tour after receiving fire while parachuting from a helicopter.

Lew even got involved in some of my porn productions even though he would be very uncomfortable and self-conscious. It was hard to keep a straight face in some of our shoots, and I had to really control myself to keep from laughing.

Always looking for a way to further line his pockets, he had been involved in smuggling diamonds from one country to another. He would hide the precious stones in a cigarette box, and then try to play stupid when caught. He later got involved in money laundering, but paid a terrible price when he was caught at the Turkish border carrying an excessive amount of currency. He spent several months in prison and almost died from malnutrition and disease. His companion was a professional singer who managed to scrape up two hundred grand over six months in order to bribe corrupt Turkish officials who finally released him from prison.

We spent a considerable amount of time in Mexico, where he continued dealing in currency and investing in real estate. I lived in a constant state of anxiety since he would often carry fifty to sixty grand in his underwear. We performed one or two shows a night in a comedy routine called Circus Circus Bang Bang at the Hilton Continental in Mexico City and we later played at the Convention Center in Acapulco. Lew was completely fluent in Spanish but I only managed to learn a few phrases. In one of my acts I had to memorize and deliver several lines in Spanish without understanding either what I was saying or what my partner was saying. Despite this handicap, my lines received uproarious laughter from the audience.

Our relationship lasted twelve years and I was married to him for six of those years. I was never married to any of my husbands for the ten years required to receive half of their social security benefits. However, I did have my only child from this marriage. Overall, Lew was not a very good father, but he did help out quite a bit when my daughter Glennel was an infant. In fact, he probably changed more diapers than I did.

He could be quite short on patience, becoming frustrated when Glennel was unable to solve some rather difficult math problems that he presented to her when she was only two years old.

Lew began to display more and more unusual behavior. He paid five grand to join a cult founded by the famous anti-tax advocate, Irwin Shiff. Even though Shiff had ended up in prison for tax evasion, Lew would not listen to reason. When my father failed to convince him otherwise, I began to file my tax returns separately.

Even more bizarre, Lew spent fifteen grand on an electronic device that was touted to cure any ailment ranging from aids to the common cold. After a few doses of electric shock treatment, he displayed considerable memory loss. At first, I wasn't sure whether or not he was just putting on an act so I took the advice of Lew's friend, Frankie Magran, and put him to the test. I brought him to upscale Nieman Marcus, and suggested that he loved to spend money. He had been an incurable cheapskate all of his life, so when he continued to fork over thousands in cash, I realized that he really had lost his mind. He gradually recovered his memory after a week in the hospital.

He may have recovered his memory, but this did not mean that he had regained his senses. He suddenly stopped paying all of the bills including essential utilities even though he could have easily afforded it. It was all part of a devious strategy to force me to continue working in order to earn enough to cover the shortfall. After this nonsense went on for several months, I contacted the District Attorney who proceeded to evict him from our home over his strenuous objection. My daughter was very much relieved to be rid of him since she had become worn out by the constant bickering between us.

When I filed for a divorce, my attorney requested a standard $5000 retainer. At the time, I considered this to be an excessive amount, never realizing the enormous amount of time and expense that this divorce would eventually cost. This case didn't take the usual eight weeks but dragged on for a frigging eight years. I became extremely frustrated and took it out on my Mormon lawyer who was a sober man doing a decent job against formidable opposition. On one occasion when I was busy, my parents went to see my lawyer bringing along my six year old daughter, looking so cute in her braided pigtails. When my lawyer asked them to wait outside because he was with another client, she innocently informed the legal secretary who also happened be my lawyer's daughter, "He doesn't look like a dumb shit to me." Glennel was just mimicking what I must have repeated dozens of times – beware of what you say around little kids.

I desperately tried to end all of this after four years of proceedings, but he would continue to throw more and more paperwork at us. His attempt to hide assets by placing them into a series of phony trust funds was also a persistent problem. I finally ended up with our $200,000 house, but my parents spent at least $300,000 covering my attorney's fees by selling their home in Nantucket. In fact, Lew threatened to break my father financially but my father replied that it would be "over his dead body." Unfortunately, my father did endure an enormous amount of stress. Lew even threatened to place Glennel in an orphanage by claiming that both of us would be unacceptable parents. The divorce cost Lew at least half a million in legal fees and court costs but he never paid his lawyer a substantial portion of it. He was definitely hit hard financially but it didn't seem to bother him and he still remained quite wealthy.

Even two years after the divorce, he would not stop the harassment and hired detectives to pursue me into California. I was forced to move because Lew managed to get me blacklisted from all the casinos and hotels in Nevada. At the time, my daughter was enrolled in Steven S Weiss elementary school in Beverly Hills where the children of many Hollywood celebrities such as Bill Cosby also attended. It would eventually cost me fifty grand to get permission from the court to live outside of Nevada.

As part of the settlement, Glennel had to fly back to Nevada every two weeks to spend time with Lew and his girlfriend. She would always complain that they were being mean to her. Since there was nothing that I could do about it because it had been ordered by the court, I suggested that she sit in the corner and read a book. Fortunately, this awkward arrangement soon ended when Lew decided to give up all parental rights which meant that he was not even allowed to write or phone either me or my daughter. Unfortunately, he never sent child support either.

Glennel Trying to Fill My Shoes

My daughter never saw him again until she made a surprise visit to his home at the age of nineteen on a Friday
evening while on vacation in Las Vegas. Their encounter resembled a bad knock knock joke. When she rang his doorbell,
he inquired, "Who is it?" She replied "This is Glennel." He
responded, "Who is Glennel?" She answered, "This is Glennel
your daughter!"

In recent years, he occasionally sent a card or even a gift on
her birthday. Glennel managed to track him down and arrange

a second meeting after six years had passed on Labor Day weekend.

This time when she knocked on the door of his Las Vegas home, she was surprised by his friendly greeting, "Glennel, it is so good to see you again," acting as if there had always been a normal relationship between them. He appeared to be in quite good health for a man in his eighties, but has recently and unexpectedly passed away. He left behind a large estate including a multitude of properties in Las Vegas. A very contentious lawsuit is currently being contested between Glennel and his long time live in girlfriend over his estate.

There have been a host of candidates for number eight. When I left Lew and moved to Beverly Hills, I began a romantic relationship with producer, Jay Harvey. To my regret, I declined his marriage proposal and he has never forgiven me. I have mentioned my long and stormy relationship with casino mogul, Bob Stupak, who proposed on more than one occasion, but I never accepted. Over the years, I have dated dozens of other suitors, but it is hard to envision any of them as one of the Magnificent Eight.

The Nifty Fifties

MY INITIATION INTO the porn business was largely by chance and not by design. I had considered taking the plunge into X rated films on the advice of my good friend Jack Palumbo, but had done nothing about it for an entire five years. He insisted that I could make up to $5000 per week as a porn star, which was three times more than I was currently making as a singer and dancer, due to the high overhead in expensive costumes.

Ironically, Jack was with me on the day that it all got started. We had just parked our car in a Las Vegas shopping mall and began walking toward the Sears store when Jack was almost hit by another car. I stammered, "Honey, watch where you are going. That car almost hit you." The driver was a gorgeous woman with long black hair who rolled down her window and in a sultry voice purred,

"Hello Jack, what are you doing?" I was quite shocked and maybe even a little jealous, wondering how a woman in Las Vegas would know a man who lived in Detroit. Jack eagerly replied, "Why Jane, how are you doing?" The mystery woman was Jane Hamilton, who was better known as popular 70's and 80's porn star Veronica Hart. I inquired, "Well Jack, are you going to introduce me, hurry up?" He announced, "Jane, this is Patty Wright. She is a big star here in Las Vegas and has been a singer and dancer in all the shows for many years." Jack went on to say that I had always wanted to make X rated movies and that I already had a considerable fan base. Jane then graciously offered the names of several agents in New York and Los Angeles which I frantically wrote down on a piece of scrap paper. In addition, she promised to call all of them on my behalf as soon as she returned home to New York.

Porn Star Veronica Hart

In the following days, I met with at least twenty-five agents. Incredibly, within a month of our meeting in the parking lot, I had signed a two-year contract for $20,000 with Caballero, the biggest company in the porn business at the time. None of the actors ever shared in the profits of the film, but were only paid a salary. I wasn't even required to do any auditions. I also didn't require any cosmetic surgery since I already had my first breast enhancement in 1969, and six other operations were to follow. I decided not to use an agent because, from experience, I had learned that most of them were not well informed and usually screwed things up. I even paid them to stay out of my way. However, today almost everyone has an agent.

Veronica, who had the classic beauty of Helen of Troy, may not have launched a thousand ships, but she definitely did launch my long career in pornographic films. She had been born and raised in Las Vegas into an affluent middle class family - her father worked at the nearby Nevada Test Site. She majored in theatre at the University of Nevada and became involved in the local theatre scene. After working as a model in England for three years, Jane moved to New York with a legitimate casting director. After two music deals fell through, she was forced to earn a meager living as a secretary.

Becoming completely disillusioned with the legitimate acting business, she was persuaded by her lover and landlord, Roy

Stewart, to give the porn industry a shot. In the 70's and 80's, most porn films had well developed story lines requiring some acting ability, so the transition was not all that radical. However, Jane decided to do some live sex shows in front of an audience before making her first hardcore film, *Fascination,* in 1960, as Veronica Hart. Her ability to enjoy sex in front of a camera made her a star in the business. In 1982, she began working behind the scenes as a director for the Playboy Channel and later directed such notable films as *White Lightning* starring Ginger Lynn. She even appeared in some mainstream plays and movies. Jane has remained a supporter of the porn business and unlike some other porn stars, has never regretted her decision.

I continued to live in Las Vegas even though all of the films were made in Hollywood. I was put up in first class hotels and given a generous expense account which included food and travel allowances, in addition to my salary of $1500 a day. Even though the workday was a full twelve hours spent mostly in makeup, my actual screen time was only a few minutes, with the dialogue usually recorded separately. It would take about thirty minutes to an hour to complete a full scene and never more than three takes, unlike a mainstream movie that may require up to a hundred takes. An entire movie would take only two to three months to shoot.

Bar Scene in *Bodacious TaTas*

My first movie, *Bodacious Ta-Tas,* produced by Swedish Erotica and distributed by Caballero, had a big budget of $250,000 and a well written script. My first scene was extremely difficult and harder than anything I had ever done. The "closed set" had a crew of several persons including a light man, a sound man, a director, an assistant director, and maybe even a crew pretending to work on the set hoping to catch a glimpse of the action. My only other similar experience was performing in amateur videos with my husband Michael Flores, who got me involved in some swinger parties. Any hanky panky off screen was frowned upon for a very practical reason - the guys were required to perform on cue. One of the male stars, Ron Jeremy, was not very nice and he went out of his way to frighten and intimidate me. He teased, "How old are you really." After the shoot he asked, "Would you like to have a ride

99

home." I replied, "No, thank you. I already have a ride home with the assistant director."

Ronald Jeremy Hyatt was born in Queens to an upper middle class Jewish family – his father was a physicist and his mother was a book editor and linguist. His uncle was the black sheep in the family having ties to Bugsy Siegel. Ron had an unusually high level of education for a porn star, earning a Bachelor's Degree in Education and Theatre and a Master's Degree in Special Education from Queens College. After a short teaching career and a failed attempt at a legitimate acting career on Broadway, he decided to give adult films a try to the consternation of his father, who warned him never to use the family name again. He went on to become the biggest male porn star in history, appearing in more than 2000 films. I would perform as his co-star in many of these films, and we eventually became good friends. We even collaborated on a film at my home in Malibu in exchange for a pool that he built for me.

At 30, I started making adult films at a much older age than the typical actress who usually started at 18 and burned out in only two or three years while being strung out on drugs. I quickly became close friends with Kitten Natividad, who was almost my same age. She met me for the first time on the set, but was familiar with my work in Burlesque and my well chronicled reputation for always landing a well heeled man. Kitten was also attracted to men with a lot of money, but refused to date a porn star explaining, "Who wants to date a slut!"

Kitten and I were required to do a girl-girl scene and we were quite nervous about it at first, breaking the tension by telling some off-color jokes. However, we were not well liked by management because we were not receptive to doing every sex act they suggested, unlike the younger girls who were open to almost anything.

I learned my lines to a tee, unlike Kitten who forgot many of her lines, but was allowed to ad lib because she had achieved stardom. The fans liked to see us together in films because we enjoyed each other's company and we were both "big titted broads who enjoyed life" as she was fond of saying. She often complained about having to do all of the heavy sex scenes while I just bounced around the set. She wined that I always had an excuse for not doing a particular sex scene, while she was being banged for hours by a big schlong.

Kitten was born as Francesca Natividad in Cuidad Juarez, Mexico, just across the Rio Grande, but moved to El Paso with her mother and eight other siblings at the age of 10. She ended up working in LA as a maid for actress and nude model, Stella Stevens, at her home in Coldwater Canyon. She would answer the door in a white uniform to welcome stars like Warren

Beatty and Linda Evans to lavish parties, wishing that she herself would someday be a movie star. She even worked as a key punch operator for IBM before she realized she could make a much better living as a stripper. In 1969, after her first breast enhancement, she began stripping under her stage name Kitten because she was small and shy. She was well known for an innovative routine taking a shower inside an oversized champagne glass.

She won the Miss Nude Universe title in both 1972 and 1973 where she caught the eye of movie mogul, Russ Meyer, and they remained together for fifteen years. She openly admits that she displayed only two talents in the competition and they were both right out front. In 1976, she performed and narrated his film *Up!* and appeared in many of his subsequent films starring in *Beneath the Valley of the Ultra-Vixens*. In 2002, after she had retired from porn films, she appeared in a mainstream film, *Night at the Golden Eagle*. She does not have fond memories of this film because she played a seedy looking bag lady on Skid Row and "made up to look ugly."

My friendship with Kitten has continued for over thirty years and she often refers to us as the "breast of friends." We have collaborated on a number of adventures including a trip to Europe several years ago. Kitten had a convention date in England and we appeared together around the country. We then traveled to Amsterdam, but because I dragged along so much heavy luggage, we had to take the train and didn't arrive there until late at night. We were only able to find a room on the thirteenth floor of a hotel with no elevator, so we had to carry all of my luggage up all of those stairs. The furnace didn't work and we were forced to eat in the cold and dark. Next day, while viewing the sights along the canals and the hookers advertising their wares in the windows, some anonymous resident recognized us. He invited us to stay at his elegant home in a fashionable part of the city, and I even considered living there permanently.

In later years, Kitten had a brief affair with my ex-husband Michael Flores, and I returned the favor by going on a date with her long-time companion, Russ Meyer. Unfortunately, he was suffering from dementia at the time and exhibited panic attacks. This was a tragic end to a long and successful career as a photographer and film maker that spanned half a century. He gained a reputation as a glamour photographer doing shoots for Playboy in 1955, but he is best known for his numerous adult films including *Vixen* and *Beyond the Valley of the Dolls*. Despite low budgets, these films earned millions at the box office.

In 1984, I appeared in my second adult film, *Stiff Competition*, which featured almost every top porn star at the time. I played Patty Cakes, one of the four girls in a blow job competition offering $50,000 in prize money. Ron Jeremy played the role of Mr. Head, the head judge, and I did what was necessary to get to the head of the class.

On Set with Ron Jeremy in *Stiff Competition*

With a huge $400,000 budget, it was the most expensive pornographic film of that era, exceeded only by *Caligula*, written by Gore Vidal, directed by Bob Guccione, and produced by Penthouse International in 1979. This lavish extravaganza, based on the life of one of Rome's most decadent Emperors, featured a surprising number of established actors including Peter O'Toole, John Gielgud, and Helen Mirren.

The following year, I became a columnist for Cheri magazine out of New York using the title, "Patty Wright, Bodacious Beauty." For a number of years, I wrote highly erotic and detailed accounts of my steamy sex scenes in my porn films. I also reported on my swinger lifestyle, and answered some incredibly intimate questions from my readers who were trying to improve their sex lives.

Meeting with the Editor of Cheri Magazine in 1985

For example, I was frequently asked, Patty, how would you describe your idea of a perfect night with a man? I would respond, first a perfect night requires a very special man. For me, that is one who is kind and witty. I like a man who politely opens a door, can strike up a good conversation, and has a good job – better yet, doesn't have to work at all!

Once I have my special man, it's important that the surroundings and the mood be just right. If we are going to dinner that evening, I want it to be a French restaurant with a strolling violinist. After dinner, we would stop in the lounge area and have a cocktail around a soothing fireplace. Once we had established the right mood for love and returned home, I am sure my special man would slowly undress me in the bedroom as I slipped out of my cocktail dress. He'd disrobe himself and lay me back in the bed. As he gently touched my pussy, he would run his tongue across my clit to make sure I was paying attention. I would beg him not to stop.

By now I would be burning with passion and lust, and it would be time to prepare for the main event. If a man is turned on, I know he will do a good job on me. I would tickle his balls! I would carefully slip my mouth over the head of his cock and roll my tongue in circles. Then it would be "down the hatch." His cock would grow larger and larger. I would crave to swallow the whole thing.

Now, if I had done my part well, he'd roll over and stick me with that long wet noodle. It would be "love at first poke." When my man does a good job, I get so wonderfully wet!

Now if you think I've told you everything I'd do on the "perfect night," you are mistaken. You can just use your imagination to dream about what would happen for the next three hours of ecstasy!

Another fan from Texas wrote that just by reading one of my articles, he had been turned on beyond belief. He could only imagine what I could do for him in person. He then went on to say, If you are ever down this way, give me a holler. and I will treat you to a night that we will never forget. We'd start with a nice dinner somewhere in downtown Houston, and then I would take you to a rodeo where I would win the prize money for you. Afterward, we would go out for a little dancing at Gilley's Club, the biggest and best honky tone in all of Texas. We'd have a few margaritas, and then off to a hotel for an evening of pleasure. I would slowly undress you kissing every part of your body as I go. Remember, everything is bigger in Texas. Write real soon. Signed, Easy Larry. I replied, Dear Easy, the favor would definitely be returned. I adore Texas studs, and I particular adore your description of our evening. My Texas fans have made many of my tours quite successful, and I am planning on returning this spring. A couple of my favorite clubs are Dallas Show World and Dream Street. I will send you my itinerary for the spring and summer, and hope that you are not tied up at the time.

Because of my exposure as columnist at Cheri magazine, I gained an enormous amount of publicity, and appeared on the cover of so many of the top men's magazines that I dominated newsstands from coast to coast and around the world. With the financial support of my husband Lew Warren, I capitalized on my fame and developed a lucrative mail order business.

Expose

Gent August 1987

Gem

Juggs November 1988

In order to meet my fans around the country, I made personal appearances in places like O'Farrell Theatre in San Francisco, Admiral Theatre in Chicago, and Show World in New York. Each location offered a unique combination of decadent pleasures. For example, O'Farrell Theatre offered four large showrooms featuring beautiful girls, an S & M room, and a special room where you could use your flashlight to play "lights man." After my own performance every night at the O'Farrell, I held a picture taking session. I let my fans pose with me while I was nude so that they could take their very own Polaroids. Priceless momentos!

Performing at the O'Farrell Theatre

The Next Night

and the Following Night

The Best Night of All

One night, a good-looking guy told me that he had seen me in Vegas several years ago, and that together. we should paint the town of San Francisco. He seemed nice and also very sexy so I agreed. I got into his car and we headed across the Golden Gate Bridge. Somehow, we managed to get stuck in a thirty minute traffic jam in the center of the bridge! It was almost as if he had planned it because the view of the ocean was breathtaking to behold. In such a romantic setting, I could not resist his advances. He pulled my seat down, and jumped on top of me. Since I do everything better with an audience watching, I proceeded to give the best oral sex show of my life. Coming up for air, I noticed at least six voyeurs peering through the window. Being the lady that I am, I wiped my face off and then took a blushing bow.

Golden Gate

I shared with my readers all of the crazy happenings that occurred during my week's engagement at the O'Farrell Theatre. My wonderful boyfriend bought me a red car which I wanted to drive and show off, so I took my manager, Lou, and travelled into the beautiful countryside. Our first stop was a lonely diner. When I went inside, I was surprised when an attractive couple approached me and asked if I was appearing in the X-rated film *Bodacious Ta-Tas*. They then invited me to sit with them at the counter. I was excited because I had developed a liking for both men and women for variety.

The young woman, who was sitting next to me, gave an alluring look, and finally asked if we would join them in their motor home for coffee. I definitely knew what she wanted. I was hoping that I could get away from my manager for a while, so that I could play games with this sweet horny thing, erotic games. As all four of us walked to her motor home, she told me in her sweet Southern drawl that her name was Jenny. Once inside, she put the coffee pot on the stove, and asked if she could show me something in her bedroom. Once we left the guys, she slipped off her jacket and exposed her bare breasts. They were almost as large as mine! She asked if I liked them and wanted to touch them. I couldn't resist and they felt so soft and warm as I caressed them. Then her lips met mine. What a wonderful feeling! She put her tongue in mine and we French kissed for a long time.

I hardly knew this girl and we were about to make love in her motor home! I wanted her so much, but all I cared about was not getting caught by her hubby. Jenny assured me that her husband Mike would entertain my manager, Lou. She told me that she always wanted to star in a porn film. I replied that she would first have to audition with me to get a part as I grinned provocatively. In response, she pulled down her tight jeans to expose her incredible body. She had a terrific tan except for her bikini areas. She had dark brownish-black hair down to her waist. Any man would have loved to be in my position. I informed her that in porn films we do anything possible of a sexual nature. At that point, she pulled out of a drawer the largest, thickest dildo I had ever seen, and began to pleasure herself. Jenny started to squirm and I became very aroused. She then screamed, and suddenly Mike and Lou came rushing into the room. She just laid there, moaning and looking adorable. Everybody laughed and applauded. It was a real blast.

Lou had to leave to make my engagement, so we were back on the road again. We soon checked into the beautiful San Francisco hotel where I had booked a suite. My manager stayed at the front desk to take care of business, while a hunk of a bell captain grabbed my bags and accompanied me to the elevator. He started to check me out. How I would have loved to grab his cock before we reached my floor. I wonder how he would have reacted.

This experience then took a wild turn. When I opened the door, he was still standing there. My cat, Susie, bolted out of the room into the hall and was lost. I started crying because she was very important to me. He ran after her and within a few minutes brought her back to me. I wanted to reward him, so I invited him into my suite for a drink. He told me that his name was Peter and that he was fresh out of high school. Well, well, well! Then the handsome devil told me that he was fan of mine and very excited to be near a real live porn star. I knew what I had to do. As my blouse dropped to the floor, I noticed that his eyes almost popped out of his head. Peter unzipped his fly and he began to stroke his namesake until his cock stood at full attention. He then grabbed me, laid me back against the couch, and began kissing me passionately. He unhooked my bra and my boobs slipped into his face so he started to kiss and suck them. My nipples got hard and I was filled with lust! He started to press his body against mine. I still had my skirt on as he rammed his huge cock inside me. Since I never wear panties, he was able to penetrate me easily. He was so big that my eyes rolled around in my head. I hoped that he would never stop.

We were suddenly interrupted when my manager knocked on the door and screamed "Show Time." I would have to continue with Peter some other time, so off to the theatre I went, most refreshed.

My sexual escapades continued around the globe. I had a fabulous two-week engagement down in South America where I played at one of the biggest hotels. When I flew out of Miami,

I was hot to trot and ready to meet some new and interesting men. As I stepped into the plane, I stuck my head into the cockpit – I always like to know who's flying my plane – and noticed the sexiest blond haired Scandinavian guy I've ever seen. He politely smiled back and I decided to sit as close to the front of the plane as possible. Men in uniforms sure do turn me on – and this one was a well-built six-footer After the flight took off and dinner was starting to be served, the very handsome blond captain came back to my seat and asked if I would enjoy having my dinner with him and his co-pilot. I gave him a smile. I couldn't accept fast enough, and I was soon sitting next to him up there in the cockpit. I decided to whip out my own private pilot's license to proudly show them. But when I looked up, it became clear to me that they were both more interested in my physical assets than in my flying abilities.

The pilot kissed me on the neck, and my pussy started to drip with anticipation. As I began to sip my champagne, I also touched his big hard on, located in the center of his fancy uniform pants. He quickly handed over the controls to his co-pilot and turned to me to lay on the biggest, sexiest kiss that I had ever received.

As I proceeded to rub his throbbing manhood, he unzipped his fly and commanded "Suck my cock" in a stern voice. I could do nothing less than swallow his cock and go into action. I immediately started deep throating his wonderful organ, from the head all the way down the shaft to the base.

When he was deep inside my throat I was afraid to gag, but I didn't really care. I wanted it all! I didn't even care that the co-pilot was watching us. After all, I'm used to having an audience!

He took off my blouse and started sucking my 44's. My nipples got so hard that my pussy began yearning for him. Next, he demanded that I sit on his cock.

I could hardly wait! Pulling up my skirt, I crawled onto his mountain of steel. As I was enjoying all of his ten inches, I felt a strange new sensation from behind.

Can you believe that the co-pilot had put the 727 on autopilot? His hand was brushing up and down my legs. As I pushed back, his hand slowly moved higher and higher. At this point, the cock inside me started foaming at the head and squirted inside me. What a wild time we all had! By the time we landed in South America, we were all exhausted.

In another article, I told the story of my trip to Canada in 1987. My first stop was Jason's, a classic night spot, in Windsor, Ontario just across the river from Detroit. The girls there had to be twenty of the prettiest lovelies on earth. Jason's definitely knew how to pick them. Many were bisexual. The one that I loved most was a dark haired , long legged creature with bedroom eyes. Every time she looked at me, it was like whispering, I want to fuck you. I didn't, but I did eventually fuck her husband. She was table dancing at the time, and I invited her into my dressing room.

Her name was Kim, and she told me that she loved working at Jason's, and hoped that some day she and her husband could be in the movies. Husband? Oh well, it didn't really matter because she invited me and my manager to a special party after the show. It would be a costume party for swingers. My manager wasn't really a swinger, but when I saw him sucking and fucking all of those hot women at the party, I went crazy.

Ernie, Kim's husband, wore a red leotard devil's outfit with a huge red dildo hanging out of it. He commanded me to lie down on my back, as his long tongue began to carefully lick my clit from one end to the other. My nipples stood out hard as my body started tingling. I screamed as I came, but he still would not stop. He mounted me slipping this strange dildo deep inside me. It was one of those pulsating types with sponge balls on one end. However, I soon discovered that it wasn't a dildo at all. He had painted his cock red and his balls to match.

In the meantime, my manager was sticking his cock into everything he could. I was so turned on watching my good friend enjoying himself so much. I don't know how many times he came, but he finally became exhausted. It's never boring at Jason's. It's a place that I will never forget.

Over the next twenty years, I went on to make dozens of other films and videos such as *Nifty Fifties* and *Older Women Younger Men*, along with their many sequels. Mature women became a marketable commodity in the porn business when a cougar was still just a big cat.

Older Women Younger Men

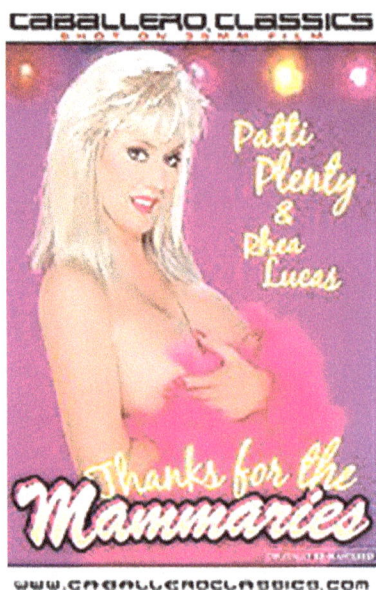

Still Hot at 52

While in my sixties, I still starred in porn films. I appeared in *Busty Mature Vixens 7,* an Elizabeth Starr production, released in 2011.

Porn actress/producer/director Elizabeth Starr was born in Las Vegas to a showgirl and a businessman. She is part English, Scottish, Italian and Austrian. Her family soon moved to Sarasota, Florida, where she grew up. As a young girl she enjoyed dancing and acting, eventually enrolling in a performing arts high school. She returned to Las Vegas to attend college, and began stripping to pay for her tuition. She later married and moved to Los Angeles, where she worked under her husband in the music industry. By her mid-20s she was divorced and back in Las Vegas where she briefly worked at a small Las Vegas record company.

She found her way into the modeling industry, with appearances in swimsuit competitions and local television commercials.

In 1995, she began posing for professional photo shoots across the US, and managed to get a photo spread in Hustler magazine. As her career in the adult-entertainment industry took off, she decided to augment the size of her breasts with string implants reaching an incredible O cup. She maintained her presence in the industry with appearances in "Score", "Gent", "D-Cup" and "Oui". As her career progressed, she began shooting more hardcore and lesbian shoots to "save her career". In 2004 Starr created her own adult movie production company, Hustler Productions, under which she directed her own movies. In 2010 she married her longtime partner, porn actor Tommy Gunn.

I was nominated for induction into the "Legends of Erotica" at a ceremony in January 2011 inside Showgirl Video in downtown Las Vegas as part of the Class of 2011. The roster of stars, recognized for their success in the adult entertainment business, had grown to over ninety, and another six were scheduled to be inducted that evening. This event, introduced in 1994 by porn advocate and guru Bill Margold, lacked the glamour and glitz of the *AVN Adult Movie Awards*, also held in Las Vegas in January, but still appealed to the multitude of porn fans in its own unique way.

Since I had come down with a bad flu and was unable to attend, I made arrangements to have my good friend Norman who lived in Las Vegas accept my award – or so I thought. When he arrived with a large poster of myself in a topless ski outfit, he was told by an angry Bill Margold that he had expected me to attend in person and would not allow me to be inducted as scheduled.

Margold went on to say that he could care less that I had given the sponsors plenty of notice and that I had prepared an acceptance speech, but would consider adding me to the Class of 2012.

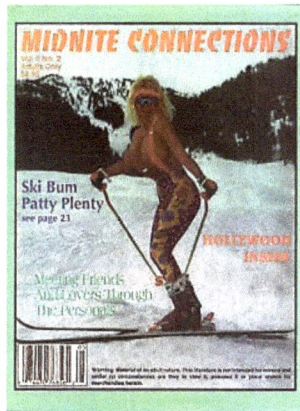

Ski the Bumps

The event was held in a large dingy room with a makeshift stage, rows of fold up chairs, and a somewhat bizarre additional attraction. Every pornstar, who had previously been inducted, had made an imprint of a body part of their choice into cement, and the impressions were used to decorate the surrounding walls.

Despite my absence, the show would go on. Margold, who resembled a rusty haired version of Teddy Roosevelt, wearing an unpressed T-shirt and jeans, greeted an equally shabbily dressed audience as they shuffled into the room to take their seats.

Before the main event, Margold introduced a newcomer to the business, Toni Andreas, who wore a tight dress with an incredibly short skirt, giving the audience amble opportunity to search for the hidden treasure underneath. She recited a poem full of erotic references and succeeded in establishing just the right mood.

Bill then requested donations for his pet project, PAWS (Protecting Adult Welfare), with the stated lofty goal of reforming the porn industry by banning teenage performers who were often physically and psychologically abused on the set. A glass jar was passed around, and members of the audience obediently stuffed dollar bills into it.

The diminished ranks of the inductees who appeared on stage were Lisa Ann, Jill Kelly, and Rayveness.

Lisa Ann was a stunning, hard bodied brunette, who somewhat resembled Sarah Palin. In fact, she had recently starred in *Who's Nailin' Paylin,* a movie produced by Larry Flynt's Hustler Video in October 2008. A doting and adoring boyfriend made her formal introduction.

Jill Kelly was a gorgeous, fashionably dressed blond, who had appeared in over 600 adult films over the course of 16 years, and she was next to be introduced. Her acceptance speech was more of a tribute to her four-legged friends than to the two-legged animals in the audience. She chose to make an impression of her delicate and well-manicured hands into the cement and then thoroughly removed the residue from her fingers.

Rayveness, on the other hand, presented a much bolder, much earthier image. She was a voluptuous, raven haired, Appalachian doll, introduced by none other than Ron Jeremy, who appeared as if he had just arrived from a homeless shelter and was recovering from a hangover. After receiving a fitting tribute for her twenty-year career, Rayveness decided to add some excitement to the proceedings by removing her top and pressing her ample bosom into the cement. The ever chivalrous Mr. Jeremy lent his assistance by pushing on her back to ensure a complete impression of her assets. Legions of the press corps lit up the room with the flashes from their cameras to record this historic event. During the question and answer session that followed, Rayveness stunned the audience by announcing that she would retire from the business to devote the rest of her life to charitable causes, as if appearing half naked in front of this audience wasn't charity enough.

The evening ended with the late arrival of Mr. Marcus, a black star most noted for wearing baseball caps and appearing with 101 women in a single film.

A Place in the Sun

WHEN I MOVED to Malibu from Beverly Hills, I settled into a beautiful, beautiful little two bedroom, two bath beach house right on the water. My landlord, Andy, lived in the famous Colony a few blocks away on the same street.

Wearing Formal Attire in My Malibu Home

When Kitten came over to visit, I asked her what she thought of my place and she said, "Oh Patty, I love it, I love it." She asked if we could make some money here, and I said, "Of course, Of course, and I will advertise for you too." She replied, "Oh great, Oh great. I need money, I need money." She was still drinking at the time and hadn't yet gone on the wagon, still being all fucked up. She would come over to my house, and I would have four appointments booked for the day, a thousand bucks a piece, for the both of us.

I would store a fifth of vodka in my freezer meant to last for six months. She would leave around four or five in the afternoon, and when at six, as I went to grab some ice to make a Bloody Mary, I would notice that the fucking bottle was empty, bone dry. Every time she came over, I would have another full bottle of vodka, and every time I went to make a drink, the bottle was completely empty. My first thought was that she was pouring it out to avoid the temptation, but she was just succumbing to her addiction, and didn't admit to it until she finally decided to quit drinking. I really didn't care about a ten dollar bottle of vodka, or a twenty or thirty dollar bottle for that matter, but it was becoming quite an annoying routine.

A few months went by, and I asked, "Kitten, why didn't you tell me that you knew my landlord Andy?" She said, "I don't know. I didn't want to work against you." "How could it go against me? I am renting, I pay him, and that's all." Anyway, he was about twenty years older, and she once gave him an unusual birthday present by jumping out of a cake.

Kitten was also a good friend of Elvira for many years, the so-called Mistress of the Dark, until one day she screwed Elvira's husband for whatever reason, either money or passion. However, when Elvira found out, she went bezerk, and refused to have anything to do with either Kitten or anyone who knew Kitten, including myself. Interestingly, Andy, my landlord, produced several movies for Elvira in Transylvania, the home of Dracula, with a brooding theme. Elvira turned the character she had created into a multi-million dollar business.

I had another landlord, Rob McCloud, who I actually did date for about six months, and this relationship provided a huge discount on my rent. I paid a mere two thousand a month for a fabulous expansive mansion right on the beach that could market as much as fifty grand a month. However, I would have to vacate on a split-second notice whenever a high roller decided to move in. I even got away with filming porn movies inside my rented home. Since rights to the property only extended to the high water mark, tourists would actually walk by on the beach at low tide to gaze at my house. Rob would joke that he rented to me on a "pro bono" basis. I objected, "Rob, how dare you say that, I paid you!" He laughed and said, " OK, OK , Patty." His father owned Glamour magazine and he was a very wealthy and successful commercial architect. He eventually married another sexy woman in the business who played the role of Alotta Fagina in the Austin Powers series with Mike Myers.

The best night spot in all of Malibu at that time was the Dume Room, a seedy dive on a craggy bluff called Point Dume, tucked between a tiny dry cleaners and a take-out pizza joint. It would ruin your reputation just to be seen there, but that didn't stop all the Hollywood elites, like Nick Nolte and Pamela Anderson, from showing up to mix with the waitresses and construction workers of blue collar Malibu. Rob McCloud was probably the only person in Malibu who shied away.

Step inside and there's an old wooden bar, a dozen comfortable stools, and a glittering fish tank built into the wall. There's an old pool table in back, stained but still level and playable. The juke box is crammed with great music, and there is a live band on the weekends. The drinks are strong and the bartenders are friendly. Talk to anyone and they'll talk back, buy you a beer, or offer to shoot a game of pool.

That's where I met Roy Orbison, Jr, a singer and songwriter in his own right, and we became lovers despite our age difference. I would frequently spend the night at his home and his mother would kindly serve me breakfast when I woke up in the morning.

I was a welcome guest at the Dume Room until I lost my temper and threw a bottle against the mirror. As a result, I was warned to stay away for thirty days. Undeterred, I later showed up disguised as a man, and somehow managed to get away with it. Nick Nolte also got a thirty day suspension but not for rowdy behavior. He was intensely disliked for not tipping the bartenders.

The Dume Room had a long and rich history dating back to the heyday of "the Duke," John Wayne, but finally closed in 2006.

Stepping out with Jack Nicholson at Glamourcon Convention

Dick Van Dyke was the "sweetheart of Malibu." We would have an annual charity event known as the "Pancake Cook Off," and were amazed at how many pancakes he could consume and somehow still maintain his slim appearance.

Trumpeter Herb Alpert was a good friend, and one of the most successful instrumental performers in pop history. He was a shrewd businessman who co-founded A&M Records, the most prosperous artist-owned companies ever established. From its humble origins as a company run out of his garage, A & M grew to become the world's largest independent label promoting such artists as the Carpenters, Joe Cocker, and Sergio Mendes & Brasil '66. However, Herb Alpert and his Tijuana Brass remained the label's flagship act, and popularized his Latin influenced style.

Another neighbor, Gerry Wersh, was Herb Albert's right-hand man, responsible for all of his photography and graphics. However, in the words of Kitten, Gerry was my kryptonite - not good for superman, and certainly not good for Patty - the only person who could pull me down and hurt my career. He was a blond whiz who would show me how to edit videos and photos on my computer, and in general befriend me, all the while, robbing me blind behind my back. It all depended on how much coke he had snorted that day. Strange things would happen whenever he was around, like your $2500 electric drill would be missing. If you were robbed – it was Gerry, if your camera were missing – it was Gerry. If anything bad ever happened – you guessed it – it was Gerry. I wouldn't be surprised if he had stolen Herb Albert's trumpet. One night when my laptop computer was missing, I told my good friend Jena to go to Gerry's trailer on the hill, beat on his door, and demand that he return it.

As he was coming up the driveway, she jumped on his car, forced open the car window with her fingers, and screamed, "Patty wants her computer back and I mean right fucking now!" Since he didn't even know her, he was terrified. However, he proved to be innocent when I later opened a lower drawer and discovered my prized computer. It was pretty hard informing Jena of this fact, and Gerry was furious when he got wind that I had found my computer. I told him that he was still on the hook for all the other stuff that turned up missing. In fact, when I later looked inside his garage, I not only found my electric drill, but several more of my tools as well. He was definately guilty of a lot of misdeeds and someone to watch at all times.

When Gerry was not available, I would go out with his brother. One night we were doing cocaine in the car alongside the road, but were spotted by the local cops. I told him to hide the coke in the woods before they got to us. They then approached the car in the pitch dark, put a flashlight in our faces, and asked us what was going on. We tried to convince them that we were just talking. They sarcastically told us that our eyes were bloodshot and our noses were dripping. Did we both have a cold? Did we need a Kleenex? Gerry's brother offered the fact that he was the security guard for Herb Albert, and plead with them not to arrest him because it might cost him his job, and maybe even get him deported back to Canada. Amazingly, the cops just left. If you were a rich and famous celebrity in Malibu and didn't get too far out of line, you would often get off the hook, while the tourists would have the book thrown at them. However, we were unsuccessful in recovering the cocaine in the woods because it was too dark and well hidden.

Cop Stop

I didn't always get away. I had to attend traffic school in Beverly Hills for speeding. Fortunately, I was in the same class with Robert Downy, Jr. He was a really sweet guy who has since managed to clean up his act and beat his drug addiction.

I also used to workout at the Malibu gym with Matthew McConaughey who lived just two doors away from me. At the time his career was taking off with films such as *Texas Chainsaw Massacre* and *Amistad*. He was infatuated with me, but for some reason a little intimated as well. Maybe my bust size was a bit too much for him.

Probably my closest relationship was with John Phillip Law, a Los Angeles native who starred in a number of movies including *The Russians are Coming, the Russians are Coming* in 1966 and *Barbarella* with Jane Fonda in 1968. He was very handsome, tall, and blond with steel blue eyes. We did everything together including long walks in the surrounding Santa Monica mountains and parties at the Playboy Mansion. He would even babysit Glennel while I attended traffic school. He eventually proposed to me, but I just didn't want to get married at the time. He told me that he loved me so much that he would even do drugs with me. I laughed and said, "What a silly thing to say! You don't even know if I do drugs." He countered, "I don't do drugs anymore either, but I would do them with YOU."

John Phillip Law with Patty on a Hike

I didn't always get along with my neighbors. I once lived downstairs in the same triplex with the daughter of Sam Walton, the founder of Walmart. She was a professional swimmer who proved to be dreadfully unfriendly and aloof. She even yelled at my daughter one time for no good reason. She was a miserable, rich and demanding person who never had a boyfriend despite her cute looks.

In contrast, I adored next door neighbor, Shirley McClaine. My daughter really liked and admired her as well, but my mother felt that she was a weirdo because of her strong belief in reincarnation.

Wearing Informal Attire

Enjoying the Malibu Sun

Mermaids and Sea Horses

I had two little "Jewish" cats named Henry and Isaac who were rare and expensive Asian leopard cats with marvelous multi-colored coats. In contrast, my neighbor who shared the triplex had two "Indian" cats, Totec and Maya. Henry and Isaac were so adorable that they would actually come into the shower with me to soak in the water. They were little gremlins who would frantically run up and down from room to room, and then hide under the couch when I became upset. You couldn't let them outside because they were so valuable that they would be stolen, and that is what eventually happened.

My Asian Leopard Cat Henry

This Little Piggy

I became a good friend of Hugh Hefner, being invited to all of the fabulous parties at the Playboy Mansion, a lavish gothic Tudor home in Bel-Air built in 1927. It all began when Kitten fixed me up with her ex-boyfriend and movie producer, Russ Meyer. I had met Russ earlier, and considered him to be a great guy, but unfortunately, he was beginning to suffer from dementia. I agreed to go on a date with him to the Playboy Mansion, to party and to take care of him, but I had no intention of marrying him. Kitten tried to convince me that he really needed a wife and that we would be a perfect match. In fact, she wanted me to save his business and protect it from a hostile takeover.

We did go out on many occasions and had a great time at all of the parties. However, he was completely off of his rocker. While sitting a short distance from Hefner's table, he muttered, "I hate that fucking man." I was startled and asked, "Russ, what man?" He pointed to Hefner and repeated, "I hate that fucking man." I tried to reassure him, "Hef is your friend and you are a guest at his party, honey." "Oh, oh, but I still hate him!" "No, you don't hate him, it's his birthday, come on, let's go over and say hi to him." Hugh then embraced Russ and exhuberantly thanked him for coming to the party, and Russ came back to reality by the repeated use of his name. Hef then asked, "Who is this beautiful woman you brought to the party" and he introduced me as his girlfriend Patty who is a big star. I knew that

Hefner liked cigars so I made a fancy, highly lacquered ashtray with my face and body at the base, which I presented to him as a birthday present and which he graciously accepted. I became his frequent guest in the nineties. However, I never developed a romantic relationship with him – I can't screw everybody all of the time!

**Russ Meyer, John Phillip Law, and Red Buttons
with Patty and Hef at the Playboy Mansion**

Contrary to popular belief, parties at the Playboy Mansion were not wild, free for all, swinger affairs. There may have been sex going on in some corner of the mansion, but it was between the couples who had arrived together. In fact, there was little use of drugs as well. However, expensive food and champagne were always available. These were typical Hollywood parties where hip show business people gathered to socialize. They certainly were not church socials, but not Roman orgies either.

You needed to be in show business and on the A list to be invited, like John Phillip Law, James Caan, and Red Buttons. They were all pretty people, but the women were not necessarily all young – I was in my fifties. It didn't matter if you were wealthy or in politics – you still weren't invited.

Hugh Hefner with Patty

I began a lifelong friendship with Olivia Newton-John through my daughter, Glennel, who was a close friend of Olivia's daughter, Chloe at school. All the kids would come over to my house and I would prepare snacks for them. Chloe would gush out, "Oh Patty, you are such a good cook." I said, "Chloe, I didn't cook anything, you kids did everything, but your mother has taught you Smoozing 101 very, very well." Chloe, replied, "I don't know what you are talking about, but OK." She was so very sweet. When my daughter moved to Hawaii, Olivia convinced me to move out there as well so I could be with her. I argued that I didn't have enough money but moved anyway. However, I always felt most at home in California, and never really adapted to Hawaii.

Patty and Olivia Newton-John

My daughter also knew the daughters of both Penny Marshall and Cindy Williams of Laverne and Shirley fame. I recently ran into Cindy Williams' daughter who was surprised to see me as well. Unlike some child stars, most of these kids were well adjusted and moved on to lead fulfilling lives. One exception is Redmond, the son of Ryan O'Neal and Farrah Fawcett, who led a turbulent life at home, and has battled drug addiction.

Liberal Activist Michael Moore

Actor James Whitmore at the Methodist Church

I even developed a friendship with the stars of the TV series *Hart to Hart,* Robert Wagner, known as RJ, and Stephanie Powers. In fact, I toured with them along with my boyfriend at the time, producer Jay Harvey. They were involved in an off-Broadway play, *Love Letters*, in which a successful lawyer played by RJ exchanged correspondence over a lifetime with an unsuccessful married woman played by Stephanie Powers.

Jay, Patty, and RJ

As far as the notorious is concerned, I was a friend of the owner of the Clippers, Donald Sterling, well known for his controversial comments on race relations, and his wife Shelly. On New Years Eve, I was sitting alone at Guido's, a popular restaurant in Malibu Village, and was pleasantly surprised when he told the staff to cover my tab for anything I wanted off of the menu and at the bar. Evidently, he felt sorry for me because I did not have a date. He must have really liked me because he usually stiffed all of the bartenders and waiters.

I created a number of business enterprises In Malibu. I wanted a way to profit from the thousands of fans that I had acquired over the years and so created a fan club. I picked a president for each state who would manage my affairs. In return for a hundred dollars, he would receive a Patty Plenty watch. These men would proudly display their watches to their wives and girlfriends who were not particularly impressed or amused. My fan club not only extended to Canada and Mexico but around the world as well. I was particularly popular in Germany and required a translator to read my mail. I sold a number of products including Patty Plenty T-shirts and pillow cases, and even considered sheets. I was shocked when I recently ran into a man in Vegas coming out of the Post Office who was wearing one after all of these years.

PREMIUM PERSONAL PATTY PLENTY FAN CLUB WATCHES
KEEP PATTY ON YOUR MIND

ACTUAL SIZE
LIMITED EDITION

PLENTY FANS ARE ALREADY WEARING THEM . . .

only

$37.95

Quality, Quartz - **NEW**
Thin Water-Resistant
GOLD Plated Case
with Genuine **LEATHER** Band

BE WITH THE *IN* CLUB - FIRST IN YOUR AREA TO WEAR THE
PERSONAL PATTY PLENTY
PRESIDENT'S WATCH

Detach order form and send to:
Patty Plenty 1350 East Flamingo, Las Vegas, Nevada 89132

QUANTITY

NAME

3 PHOTOS X $10.00 =
add $3.00 Shipping 3.00
TOTAL
(Nevada residents add 6% sales tax)

ADDRESS

C   STATE   ZIP

PHONE (   )

MAKE CHECKS PAYABLE TO : PATTY PLENTY
☐ CHECK OR MONEY ORDER ENCLOSED
☐ MASTERCARD   ☐ VISA   ☐ C.O.D.
CARD #

I certify that I am at least 18 years old and believe that these materials are within the "community standards" of my area.
Signature is required before shipment. SIGNATURE

Patty Plenty Fan Club Watches

150

One of the more unusual products that I sold was Patty Plenty wine. It was produced by Somerset Winery in Oklahoma outside of Tulsa. I paid about ten dollars for both red and white varieties including labels and shipping which I then sold for $19.95 by mail order. Although certainly not a top quality wine, it was generally accepted by the public.

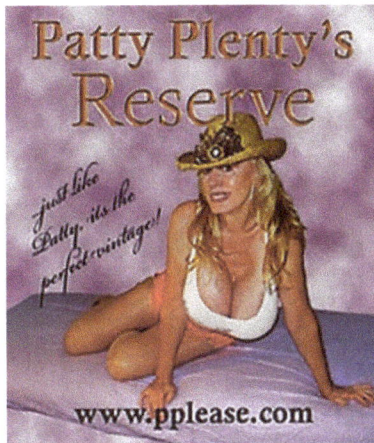

I tried to sell my wine at retail as well using a clumsy ruse in an attempt to get it accepted. I walked into Whole Foods, bought a bottle of their store brand wine, removed their label, stuck it on my own bottle, and then returned it complaining that I didn't like it.

Probably the best money making scheme of all was my breast enlargement cream. To market this product, I conjured up a story that I had traveled to a small remote village in Communist China just west of the Portuguese island of Macau while on my world tour. There I found that the local females all displayed extremely well developed breasts due to the results of using an ancient Chinese secret remedy. The young women were using a secret lotion made from local herbs that they applied to their breasts that defied nature. I claimed I had brought back a sample of the cream to the United States and hired a chemist to analyze the formula. I also claimed that I had used it on myself and increased my breast size to 44DD. It also gave me a warm sensation in my nipples and crotch. I advertised that I was offering this product to my loyal fans at only $39.95 along with a money back guarantee.

I actually used Crisco oil that could be purchased at any grocery store, pink cake, and ginseng costing a total of only twenty dollars netting a very nice profit indeed. I even got the endorsement of Dr Sinclair of Beverly Hills, a well respected plastic surgeon. The profits kept rolling in for a number of years until further sales were banned by the Federal Trade Commission. I considered challenging their ruling but I would have needed to pay a cool one hundred grand to a well-established lawyer.

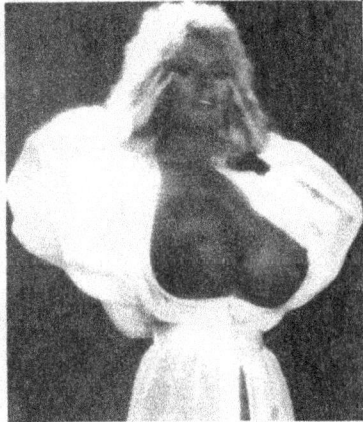

In addition, since I was using the name of Patty Plenty, I established a company called PP Enterprises which I later changed to Fanfare Studios with the purpose of producing and marketing adult videos to the general public. I had three different lines of videos – R-rated, X-rated and Custom, where for $300 you would get a half hour video of anything you wanted.

I started the business in Vegas but had a lot more success in Malibu simply because California is bigger and better. I was heavily in debt and sending my daughter to private school, so I needed to increase my income substantially. Therefore, I decided to offer massages. In order to cover my ass with the law, I required all of my clients to sign a form stating that they were members of my fan club and not in law enforcement.

PATTY PLENTY FAN CLUB

You are cordially invited to become an Honorary Member of the World Famous (44/DD-24-36) **Ms. PATTY PLENTY FAN CLUB.** Now you can keep abreast of her Latest News Events and Up/coming Live Stage Show Engagements. Your membership will entitle you to a 10% Discount on all **PATTY COLLECTABLES.**

MEMBERSHIP KIT INCLUDES:

OFFICIAL MEMBERSHIP CARD (GOOD FOR 10% DISCOUNT)
AUTOGRAPHED "NUDE" 8x10 GLOSSY PHOTOGRAPH
"PATTY CLUB" NEWS/UP-DATE

with

PATTY'S LIVE STAGE SHOW ENGAGEMENTS
PATTY COLLECTABLES CATALOG ORDER FORM

- Patty Cassettes
- Patty's Press Book
- Patty Fantasy Polaroids
- Patty Autobiography
- Patty Videos

Please, RUSH me my membership kit. I have enclosed my check/money order for $20.00 plus $1.00 postage and handling.. (Nevada residence add 6% tax.)

Name: _____

Address: _____

City:_____ State:_____ Zip:_____

Payable to PATTY PLENTY, 1350 East Flamingo 13-B/105,
Las Vegas, Nevada 89132

Old Business Card

New Business Card

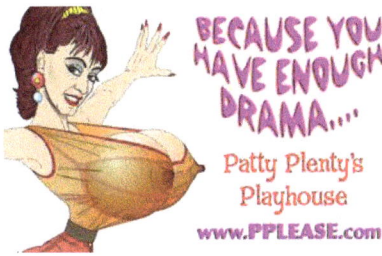

Cartoon Business Card

Matchbook Promotion

An unfortunate consequence of being in business with my husband Lew Warren was having him turn me into the IRS for tax evasion in 1983. The agents unexpectedly arrived at my door to begin a criminal investigation. The problem festered for over a decade until my federal and state tax liability ballooned to almost a hundred thousand and I was hit with a tax lien.

In an attempt to resolve this unbearable situation, I obtained the services of a highly rated accountant in Newport Beach who had a number of celebrity clients. Unfortunately, he was unable to get the IRS to review my case because my delinquent taxes were beyond the three year limit – some as old as ten years.

Just when it appeared hopeless, I finally got a break. I found out that my good friend Norman in Las Vegas had been a corporate accountant twenty years earlier. He informed me that there was a little known federal agency called the Tax Advocate Service that handled tax cases that could not be resolved by ordinary means. When we contacted that agency, they agreed to take our case but we had to submit detailed records of my business expenses for tax years 2000 and 2002. I didn't have adequate accounting records for those years but I had kept all of my receipts piled up in boxes. Norman spent months combing through the receipts and preparing a large number of spreadsheets that proved that all of my deductions were legitimate.

However, the IRS was still not satisfied. Since my expenses greatly exceeded my earnings, they disallowed most of my deductions. Fortunately, we had a meeting with an auditor in LA who was sympathetic to my plight. He accepted a letter from my deceased father showing that he had been donating money to cover most of these expenses. I was delighted when the auditor decided to remove almost the entire tax liability and the tax lien.

Even though I have lived in Hawaii for several years, I still frequently visit LA to see old friends, and to get advanced medical care. I also occasionally come to undergo cosmetic procedures from the best surgeons in the country.

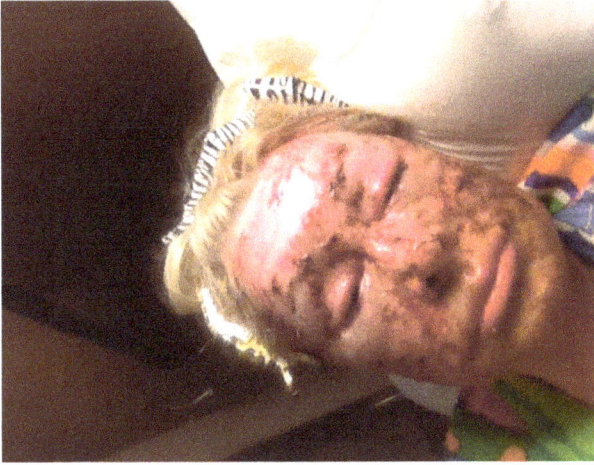

Cosmetic Surgery Horror Show

Nose Job

A Stranger in Paradise

AFTER LIVING IN Malibu for a few years, my daughter Glennel threatened to run away from home, all the way to Hawaii. Since she was only fifteen and way too young, I decided that I would have to move with her. I was making a lot of money in LA, so it was a big sacrifice for me. However, I rented a hotel room in downtown Waikiki, and used my connections in Hawaii to make a good living,

We eventually migrated to the island of Maui where I set her up with a house, a maid and a car. After she graduated from a very expensive private school, we moved back to Oahu. She went on to attend Hawaii Pacific University, and is currently a successful financial consultant, as well as an expert surfer. I bought a property in Hau'ula on the North

Shore right on Kamehameha Coastal Highway. It was a cozy
two room beach house with a good view of the ocean, even
though it was on the opposite side of the road. I eventually
painted the interior a bright yellow which exuded a cheer-
ful atmosphere. There was a large front porch and a patio in
back. Despite its small size, it quickly increased in value to
almost a million. I was sandwiched between a very small
house with a veterinarian and contractor couple on my right,
and an art studio on the left. Whenever I was out of town, I
would rent it out to tourists, and keeping it in pristine condition was quite a chore.

Vintage Pan Am Promotion

Front Porch of My Beach House

View from the Porch

Patty on Guard Duty

Chinaman's Hat North Shore

I was near the northernmost point of the island where the splendid Turtle Bay Resort was located, and also near the big waves of the world famous Banzai Pipeline. Turtle Bay Resort boasted some of the best restaurants on the island including one on the ocean where diners could be served right on the sandy beach. It was even common to catch a glimpse of President Obama at the resort.

I am often visited by friends and family from the mainland, including my mother, and my friends from Vegas, Flo and Norman. Bob Stupak was also a frequent guest, but never quite captured the Aloha spirit, not adapting to Hawaiian food and music.

Patty with Bob and Glennel at Mortons

Glennel and Patty

Enjoying the Hawaiian Lifestyle

I upgraded my popular website www.pplease.com adding some impressive audio and video, creating a Hawaiian theme. Visitors to my site are greeted by me as a Hawaiian hula dancer accompanied by some stirring Hawaiian music. My fans are kept informed of my future plans, able to purchase my memorabilia and CD's, view my thousands of photos, and even post their comments.

I developed a relationship with Buzzy Hong and his girlfriend from Maui, who had been an escort in Vegas. He was a tough Chinese-Korean former cop with political connections, who became a friend of Governor Abercrombie who I had the chance to meet. He never ran for political office himself, but was influential in putting local politicians into office.

Buzzy Hong with Patty and Governor Abercrombie

I became involved in politics myself when I helped supervise the Republican caucus in a state that was heavily Democratic.

I'M A DEMOCRAT & I'M VOTING
★T★R★U★M★P★ ©

I recently moved to one of Buzzy's properties on the South Shore east of Waikiki and Diamond Head. I worked hard to upgrade the house installing new wiring and carpeting before moving in. I rent out other rooms, sometimes charging as much as three grand a month. Life in paradise doesn't come cheap!

There are a number of celebrities from the mainland who have also made a home for themselves in Hawaii. Jim Nabors, best known for his role as Gomer Pyle, has lived there for fifty years.

I remain very active, walking several miles a day, exercising at the gym, swimming, and attending dance class with the native Hawaiians, towering over them in height. I am also active on Social Media, including Face Book, Linked In, and Twitter. I like to date younger men, getting an occasional proposal, and even taking cruises with them. However, I recently took a solo trip to Rio de Janiero and Buenos Aires to meet my South American fans

I flew from Honolulu to Vegas to Miami. Since I had a fifteen-hour layover waiting for my American Airlines flight to Rio, I rented a car and drove to visit a good friend of the family, Carolyn Dotson. She was a successful writer of several microwave cook books for Westinghouse, who lived in a beautiful home in Naples on the Gulf side of Florida.

Since I was about to take a long trip to South America all by myself, without a boyfriend or family member, I worried that I would have a hard time being alone. I chided myself for making such a big mistake, but soon realized that I had always found a way to have fun regardless of the situation.

I arrived in Rio two days early, and my first concern was finding a hotel that was reasonably priced and close to the cruise ships. I called around to various hotels but couldn't get a straight answer. It wasn't a language problem because the major hotels are fluent in English. I wanted to stay on Ipanema Beach because I love the ocean, but it was just too expensive. For example, the Marriott cost a whopping $500 a night. I therefore looked at other hotels on the beach and found one rated three stars for only $85 a night, but since I was alone, I would probably need a safer hotel.

Then I discovered a Sheraton perched on a hill overlooking the beach for $250 a night, and I couldn't have been happier. It took an hour to get there from the airport while the meter kept adding up the fare. I finally arrived at the hotel about 8 AM, well before check-in time. I was unwashed, drunk, and exhausted, needing to crash immediately. However, I was told by the front desk to relax and have some coffee while they would try to have my room ready in about an hour. To my relief, I was ushered to my room in only fifteen minutes.

Spectacular View from the Sheraton Balcony

I dragged in my bags, put on my night gown, and prepared to hop into bed. But first, I went out on the balcony to take a look, and was overwhelmed by the beauty. Even though I had not slept for three days and was dead tired, I just had to make an appearance. I took a quick shower, put on my bathing suit and slippers, and was now ready to go down to the beach. This was not Ipanema Beach, and it was fortunate for me that it wasn't. Several of the passengers on my subsequent cruise had been robbed there, including a younger man, an actor from New York, who I later befriended.

I decided to sit in a lounge chair next to the beautiful pool, carrying my blanket and towel. As I put on some lotion, I saw a guy, sitting a few chairs away, get up to take pictures. I introduced myself as Patty, and we agreed that the entire view was spectacular. He told me that he was an American who used to live here while running a big manufacturing plant, but now he came only for business. He now worked as a purser for American Airlines, and had been married and divorced twice. I exclaimed, "What a coincidence, you work for American Airlines, that is the one that I just flew in on!"

I was flattered when he told me that I was very sexy and offered to give me a tour of the beach. We found a group of young guys walking the tight rope. Some were profession- als walking high above between the hills, and some were trainees walking just a few feet above the ground. He took a picture of me with the young guys while I attempted to walk the tight rope myself for my fans. We became good friends, and he has flown me twice to Florida, putting me up in some great hotels. He has a two bedroom condo in Fort Lauderdale, and offered to let me stay there whenever I wanted to visit my fans. He would give me the run of the place when he was not home, and when he was home, we could go to the nude beach together. I didn't think that was such a good idea and said, "I get paid to take my clothes off, and now you want me to take them off for free!" It had nothing to do with modesty since I wear very sexy swim suits, both bikinis and one piece that reveal almost as much.

I had a really good time in Rio. I met a lot of men who took me shopping and to some great restaurants. Brazilian food is fantastic, as spicy as the women. Brazilian red wine is unsurpassed.

Learning to Walk the Tight Rope on a Rio Beach

I left Rio on a ten-day cruise stopping at ports and coastal islands in Brazil south of Rio, in Uruguay, and in Argentina east of Buenos Aires, where I stayed for an additional two days.

Relaxing on a Coastal Island South of Rio

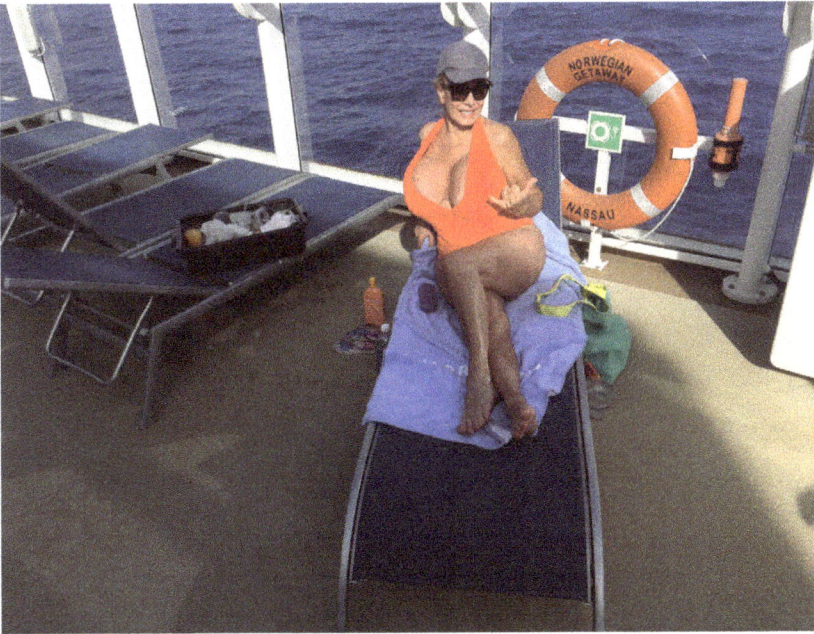

I Love Being on Deck

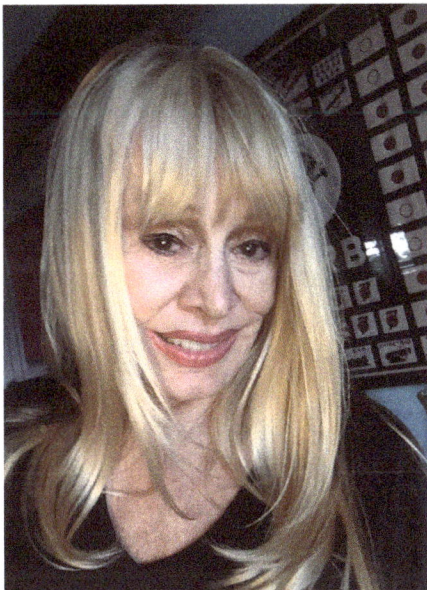

I Love Being Off Deck

Currently running in Las Vegas at Planet Hollywood is "A Tribute to the Beatles" that is receiving rave reviews. An Ed Sullivan impersonator opens the show with a funny dialogue, and then introduces a group of impersonators as the Beatles. Not only do they closely resemble the originals, but their very accurate rendition of the classic hits of the 60's, using vintage equipment, does as well.

Beatles impersonators seem to be popping up everywhere. On my cruise ship off the coast of South America, I personally met a Brazilian version.

**Patty Joins Brazil's Version of the Beatles
(photo by Carlos Munoz)**

I decided to buy the drink package because otherwise my drinks would cost twenty dollars each. I came out of my suite, went to one of the bars and a young guy says, "Wow, can I buy you a drink?" I went to another bar on the ship, and the exact same thing happened, but this time I asked for expensive champagne. In only a couple of days, I had collected five guys from bars all over the ship.. The game was up when one of these guys asked me if I had a drink package. He was pretty upset when I told him that I did, because his drink package didn't cover my drinks, and he had rung up a hefty tab. Fortunately, he told me, "Patty, I still love you, and I am still willing to take you shopping and to dinner, but I won't buy you any more drinks." It seemed that all of these guys were from New York, and had left girlfriends behind, so I had all of these good looking young guys all to myself.

After a long cruise, I arrived in Buenos Aires, the beautiful capital of Argentina, resembling a large European city rather than one in Mexico or Central America. It was very cosmopolitan having attracted immigrants from all over Europe.

I took a number of tours, including a city tour, when I was surrounded by a swat team dressed in black and carrying guns. I was told by an American tourist from Brownsville not to take pictures of them. They would confiscate my expensive Nikon camera and even arrest me, and the American embassy wouldn't do anything for me. Not to be deterred, I took a picture of my new friend positioned in such a way that the goon squad was in the background.

I also met with my Argentinian fans who took me to all of the hot spots where we wined and dined. The dancing and the music are wonderful. After all, this the home of the Tango. The prices were a bargain, so I bought some fabulous jewelry. I regret not buying any excellent original art.

I flew back to Miami on Emirates Airlines. Calling my flight first class would be a gross understatement. The luxury of this airlines is portrayed in the movie, *Sex in the City*, in which the actresses flew to Abu Dhabi in the United Arab Emirates on the Arabian Peninsula. I had my own suite with a cabana bath, a bed, a television, and even my own mini bar. I didn't have to share with anyone. Finally, I flew from Miami back to my home in Hawaii on American Airlines.

This was not my first trip to South America. In December, 1978, just a month after the mass suicide in Jonestown in northwest Guyana, I had performed in a big show in Georgetown, the capital of Guyana, as well as in Parimaribo, the capital of neighboring Surinam. I had been hired by Televisa, the biggest television company in all of Mexico, to perform in Mexico City because they really liked my show at the Fountainbleu in

Miami. They were so pleased with my Mexico City success that I was given a contact to work in South America as well.

I also toured the former notorious prison on Devil's Island off the coast of French Guyana portrayed in the movie *Papillon*. I took a side trip to the remote jungle interior where I dined at a restaurant with my husband that was so remote that it attracted very few customers. Therefore, it needed to charge outrageous prices to anyone hardy enough to venture there. In fact, it cost us $150 apiece just for the meal. Finally, I took a dugout canoe in the Amazon rain forest where the guide shot an alligator for me. In most countries, alligators are a protected species, but are allowed to be hunted in South America where they are so plentiful. I had to fill out a mountain of paperwork to get permission to import the carcass to Miami, but it was confiscated by one of the legal authorities, even though I had gotten approval.

Shortly after my flight to Rio and my cruise to Buenos Aires, I decided to take a cruise to Cuba with my mother. In the short period of time that Americans have been allowed to visit, the island has been transformed. They are joining the multitude of vacationers from Canada and Europe.

We spent four days in Cuba. I would leave the ship and walk an average of ten miles a day all over Havana, while my mother stayed on the ship, looking out from the dock. On our last day, I convinced mother to leave the ship to take a two hour tour of the city in one of those remodeled old American cars. I told her that since she could drink and raise hell, she was able to come ashore. Getting her off the ship was no easy task because we had to take her cart and walker through several layers of security. I even boarded the wrong ship in all the confusion.

Mother and Daughter as Drinking Buddies

Touring Havana with Mother

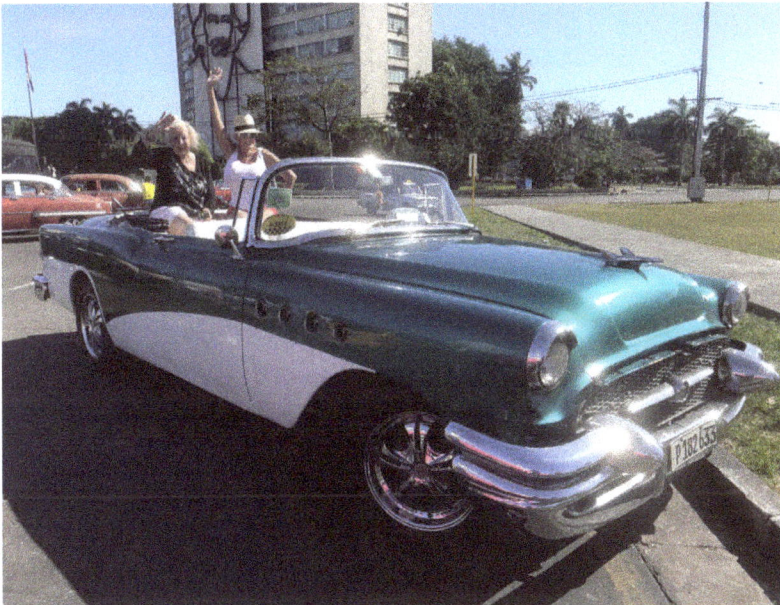

Full View of this Remodeled American Car from the Fifties

Classic Old Buildings in Havana

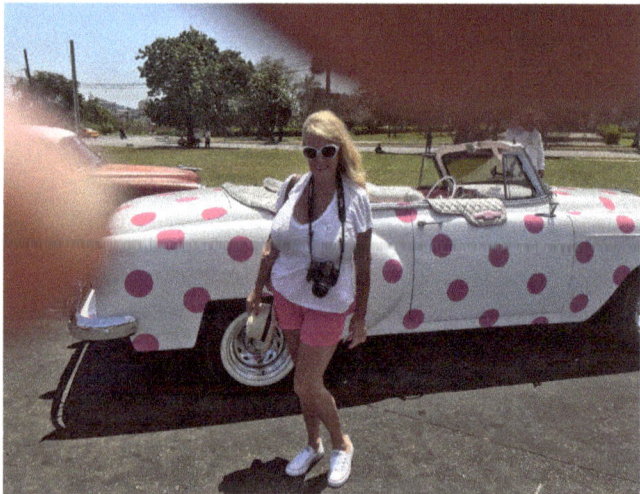

Why Not Polka Dots?

I met a driver who told me through a beautiful young interpreter, "I never made more than twenty dollars a month, but now I make as much as seven hundred every week. Yes, I do love the Americans!" A big gap has long existed between the very rich and the very poor in Cuba, although greatly modified by the Revolution at the cost of personal freedom. Today, a new gap exists between the poor and the newly rich.

Cubans still drive old American cars, but most of them have new engines and white leather interiors. The exteriors are painted in bright and unusual colors. There are some new cars around from Europe but they are very expensive.

I had seen the Caribbean Coast of South America and the Atlantic Coast, so I decided to see the Pacific Coast as well. However, this time I wanted to have a companion. I asked a male friend but he declined because he didn't like South America, and then asked my good friend Flo who also declined because it would be just too expensive. Finally, I asked my mother who complained that she was too old, and besides, whenever she went on a cruise with me, we always ended up fighting. Since we would be traveling on a huge Norwegian cruise ship, I promised that if we ever got into an argument, I would go to the opposite end of the ship for two hours, and not return until we had both calmed down. In addition, if I took this cruise, I would qualify for Platinum status and get a lot of perks, including free rooms, gourmet dinners, and even expensive champagne. In effect, I would be treated like royalty. I made such a good case for myself that she finally agreed to go with me. In early December, 2017, we left Miami, slipped through the Panama Canal, and headed to the Pacific Coast of Colombia, Ecuador, Peru, and finally Chile.

In order to transit from the Atlantic to the Pacific, it was necessary for our cruise ship to pass through the 50 mile long Panama Canal. Despite our ship's large size, it was able to pass through due to a recent project to expand the width of the canal. The passage normally takes 8 to 10 hours depending on the volume of maritime traffic. The canal has two lanes going in opposite directions, with six locks for each lane that adjust the water level to match the elevation of the surrounding terrain. I even received a certificate once I completed the passage.

Wearing Panama Hat on Cruise Ship

The Love Boat

I had a strange encounter with a very short, very rich, eccentric man named Steve, who wore lots of very expensive jewelry. He approached me and exclaimed, "You are the most beautiful woman in the world!" After a short conversation and subsequent meetings, I was completely stunned when he offered me a $70,000 diamond studded "engagement" watch. He was extremely wealthy, maintained three very expensive homes around the world, and he had a background as an orchestra conductor. Despite his diminutive size - just 4' 10", he exhibited a gigantic ego by constantly trumpeting his perceived accomplishments in life.

We remained companions throughout most of the cruise, until we had a falling out over his refusal to follow up with an engagement ring. My mother was greatly relieved because she considered him to be way too short and highly annoying.

The Three Matineers

When we arrived in Lima, the beautiful capital of Peru, I decided to explore the city on my own, rather than take one of the tours. This proved to be a bad mistake because I quickly became lost in a city where few residents understood English, not even the business class. When I used the word "puerto" to communicate that I wanted to return to the ship, it was interpreted as airport where I was driven to by mistake. In desperation, I resorted to pantomime. I made a flying motion with my arms while shaking my head to indicate no airport. I then made a swimming motion with my arms while nodding my head to indicate ocean. Nothing seemed to work and I was close to tears. By a stroke of luck, I somehow found a police chief who spoke perfect English, but unfortunately my cruise ship would soon leave port. Incredibly, he was so sympathetic to my plight that he rushed me to the waiting ship in a police escort worthy of a visiting head of state.

We went on to the north Chilean port of Arica located in the extremely dry Atacama desert. Our final destination was Santiago, the capital of Chile, where mother and I boarded a flight back to Miami. After missing a connecting flight, we eventually made it to Tulsa where I dropped her off. I went on to Las Vegas to celebrate New Year's Eve, and then back to Hawaii.

On April 28, 2018, I reached the golden age of 70, but I am just getting started. I just returned from a trans-Atlantic voyage from Miami to Southampton, England with a writer from Marco Island, Florida. We then visited the coast of Portugal and flew off to Paris. Finally, I went all the way to China. When I returned to Hawaii, I had travelled around the globe.

I am even considering performing in a one woman show in Las Vegas called *Patty Plenty Live,* so I can tell the story of my long and tumultuous career in which there was never a dull moment.

www.ingramcontent.com/pod-product-compliance
Lightning Source LLC
Chambersburg PA
CBHW040412110426
42812CB00033B/3355/J